Contents

Introduction

Sopwell Residents Association (SRA) was founded in 2003 and has been working hard since its inception to engender pride in the area. Sopwell is often seen as deprived, with more than its fair share, according to the national average, of local authority owned properties and a larger than average proportion of residents from multi-ethnic communities, a fact which Sopwell residents generally see as an advantage. Sopwell is also a very beautiful area and we want to keep it that way.

This publication started as a modest project, called the Sopwell Project, to find out about Sopwell's history. A group of us wanted to show the rest of St Albans how attractive Sopwell is with its many green spaces and a large stretch of the river Ver. Our aim was to map the environment to show how it has changed over the years. Apart from one or two areas within the Sopwell boundaries, most of the area was just a large green space until the nineteenth century, so much of its known history is fairly recent. The more we researched, the more excited we became and the outcome originally intended – printing a few leaflets and putting information on our website – was no longer enough. We felt we had to write it all down in a book, and this is the result.

In 2009 the SRA applied for, and was successful in obtaining, a small grant from the Herts County Council Locality Budget which has been spent on research in local libraries and archives, travel to other collections such as the Aerofilms collection in Swindon, subscriptions to online databases, and paying for general photocopying and printing. We also purchased a digital voice recorder to record interviews and memories of local residents. The Sopwell history project was publicised in our biannual newsletter, which is delivered to every household in Sopwell, on our website www.sopwell.org.uk, and in the *Herts Advertiser*; and, eventually, residents came forward to offer their memories.

There are numerous publications about St Albans but they include very little about the Sopwell area, apart from the Nunnery ruins, the Holy Well and St Stephen's Church – indeed many people believe that 'Sopwell' means the Sopwell House Hotel and nothing more. I have tried, therefore, to cover everything that is memorable and interesting about Sopwell. Much of the information is based on colourful recollections. I have concentrated on topics which have had very little written about them and many that have never been recorded.

Sopwell is bordered by Old London Road, Holywell Hill (from Belmont Hill southwards), St Stephens Hill and Watling Street down to the Park Street roundabout and the North Orbital as far as the mainline railway bridge, and encompasses the Cottonmill and St Julian's estates, the area to the east of St Stephen's Church, New Barnes, Priory Park, Verulam golf course and Riverside Road Fisheries. However, it has been necessary to stretch the boundaries a little further at times to include some of the interesting information found, i.e. the west side of Watling street, the north side of Old London Road and Holywell Hill just above Belmont Hill. At the time of writing, there is a possibility that Thorpe Road and part of Sopwell Lane with the Hare and Hounds public house may be included within our boundary, so completing the corner from Old London Road to Belmont Hill.

Sopwell's known history starts in medieval times with Eywood, the Holy Well and the nuns at St Mary's Priory who famously dipped bread in water (sops) from the well to give to pilgrims on their way to St Alban's shrine at the Abbey. The next major change came with the Dissolution of the Monasteries in the sixteenth century. There is another major leap into the nineteenth century with the introduction of the railways and industry. However, 'Sopwell' as we know it did not come into its own until the last century with the post-war housing boom. Although there is no exact cut off point, most of this history ends with the twentieth century.

The Sopwell Residents Association is unfunded. We have been given some money, but mainly we are relying on sales to pay for printing. If there are any profits, they will be ploughed back into the Project to benefit the Sopwell community.

Sopwell House
c.1900

600 year old oak tree on the golf course
© Sandy Norman

Chapter One
Sopwell's early history

Although Sopwell appears as a relatively modern area, there is, surprisingly, a lot of traceable medieval history. It is also a history of the appropriation of the land. What once belonged to the Church became the property of the monarchy, after the Dissolution of the Monasteries, to allocate how it wished. This took place all over Britain. All the land in Sopwell was granted to Sir Richard Lee by King Henry VIII and, over the years, has been handed down or sold to succeeding generations. Most of the land in Sopwell still belongs to the Verulam Estate.

Eywood

In medieval times, there was an area called Eywood (sometimes written as Eyewood, Eye Wood, Eywode or Ayewood). Eywood extended from where the Abbey station is now towards Park Street, so it is likely to have covered most of Sopwell. The *History of the County of Hertford* describes its limits: 'That part of the river which lay between Sopwell Mill and Stankfield Mill[1] formed the boundary on the north-east, and to the extreme south lay the hamlet of Park Street.'

The Eywood estate, which appears to have been mostly woodland, was given to the monastery of St Albans in the eleventh century by Odo, Bishop of Bayeux and half-brother to William the Conqueror. He gave Eywood in the hope of gaining favour in his quest to become Pope. He did not succeed, but his claim to fame is that he commissioned the Bayeux tapestry for his cathedral in Bayeux. In the fourteenth century there were paths both for walking and for riding running through the wood, but no record is found of any tenements there until two centuries later, when an Eywood Grange was leased to William Bayley. In the fifteenth century John Langley was appointed Forester of Eywood. The monastery held the wood until the Dissolution, and in 1540 the King granted it to Sir Richard Lee who was one of Henry VIII's military architects and rather a favourite at the court. He was also granted the Sopwell Priory lands. Lee, in turn, entrusted the estate to Richard Worsley and others for the use of his daughter Anne and her descendants, and then to Humphrey Coningsby for 48 years. The property afterwards became incorporated with the Manor of Sopwell.[2]

There was an Eywood Road which was the road running along the south side of the gasworks (now Sainsbury's in Griffiths Way). It marked the line of Eywood Lane, which was an ancient lane following the line of the borough boundary. It became a modern street at the time of the First World War.

Hugging ancient cedar in St Stephen's field
© Sandy Norman

We still have several ancient trees in Sopwell which will have witnessed our early history. These may have been part of Eywood. In 2009, the SRA recorded several ancient trees in St Stephen's churchyard and field, one of which, a cedar, is said to have been around at the time Henry VIII was courting Anne Boleyn. It is over 500 years old and measures over 9 metres in girth. There are many ancient trees in the area around Sopwell House Hotel, which was once Sopwell Park. The largest and probably oldest oak tree in Sopwell was recorded on Verulam golf course. It measures 7 metres around and is estimated to be over 600 years old.

St Julian's Leper Hospice

There was once a leper hospital in Watling Street, which was founded in the twelfth century and lasted until the sixteenth century. It is difficult to imagine, but leprosy was quite common during the Middle Ages. At one time, nearly every town had a leper hospital in its vicinity and St Albans had two.[3] St Mary's at Prae was for women and the other, St Julian's, was for men.

Abbot Geoffrey, who was the Abbot of St Albans between 1119 and 1146, founded St Julian's Hospital for Leprous Men in around 1130. It was built on a piece of land called Kingeshu, or Kingsho, and was dedicated to St Julian. It was described as being built by the side of Watling Street and near the wood called Heved or Eye Wood.[4] Abbot Geoffrey's endowment was confirmed to the hospital by Henry II (of Thomas à Becket fame), who granted the lepers one penny a day in perpetuity. From 1160 onwards, the sum of 30 shillings and five pence was paid to them annually by the Sheriff of Hertfordshire. In 1344 it was decreed that in future there should only be six lepers and priority was to be given to the monks of St Albans and those born within the jurisdiction of the Abbey. Married men were only admitted if they also adopted a religious life, so freeing the husband from the tie of marriage.[5] When St Mary's at Prae was built, c. 1194, the women lepers were separated from the men and moved there.

We can imagine a little of what the hospital building was like. On the side of the hospital facing the road there was a long walk covered by some kind of porch projecting from the building. On the opposite side of the hospital was a gate leading into the fields. There was a brewhouse, bakery, granary and a garden.[6]

The hospital declined during the fifteenth century and, in 1505, after a dispute over the mastership of the hospital, it was annexed to St Albans Abbey. In 1545, after the Dissolution of the Monasteries, the site of the hospital was granted to Sir Richard Lee and remained with his descendents until 1649. Then it was taken over by John Ellis, who demolished what remained of the hospital and built himself a house, also called St Julian's. This eventually became St Julian's Farm. One locally famous person who lived there was Henry Killigrew. He owned the estate from 1690 until his death in 1712. Henry Killigrew was an MP for St Albans between 1705 and 1708.[7] By 1820 the farm and surrounding lands had passed down to William Wilshere and his descendents. The old medieval tithe barn, originally part of St Julian's Hospice, became part of the farm. This was taken down when the Tithe Barn estate was built and is now in the Chilterns Open Air Museum.

The hospital church was on the other side of Watling Street. There is a marker which indicates this on the OS map of 1899. It looks as if it was on the corner of Vesta Avenue and Watling Street, exactly where St Bartholomew's Church is now. 'The church stood in the field on the other side of the road through which the modern pathway runs from St Julian's to the gasworks.'[8] This was described as being highly inconvenient for those walking up and down Watling Street as they were liable to meet the lepers who were going to and from the church to their daily services. The poor men had to be stopped from 'making strolling and wayward stoppings' across the road and were directed to hurry across it.[9] The lepers could also follow the service in St Stephen's Church by looking through the small hole (squint) in the Lady Chapel.

Sopwell Nunnery

In Cottonmill Lane stand the ruins of a Tudor mansion, but underneath these ruins lies another ruin, that of the medieval Sopwell Nunnery. Legend says that, in about 1140, two holy women lived as hermits beside the river. They built themselves a primitive shelter by winding branches of trees and wattles together and covering them with bark, next to the woodland called 'Eywode' not far from the bank of the river. They led a life of abstinence, vigil and prayer and lived solely on bread and water. Geoffrey, the Abbot of St Albans, was so impressed by their piety that he established a nunnery for them close by. The nunnery grew in 'spiritual and worldly prosperity'[10] and became famous for its good reputation. The nunnery followed the Benedictine order and was called St Mary's of Sopwell, which in time became Sopwell Priory. The name Sopwell came from the spring nearby in which the holy women dipped their bread or sops.

After the priory had been built, Abbot Geoffrey laid down the rule that the number of nuns living there should not exceed thirteen; this signified Jesus and his twelve apostles. He also insisted that the nuns be locked up at night to ensure their safety and for them to adhere to the strict rules of solitude and chastity. Apparently some of these rules could not have been followed very strictly because, in 1338, another abbot, Michael de Mentmore, deemed it necessary to impose a new set of rules on the inmates.[11] These stated that: the nuns should be silent in the church, cloister, refectory and dormitory; they should get up when the bell rang; they should shut the garden gate at curfew; and that any men should only work outside the nunnery.

By the time of the Dissolution in 1537 there were only five nuns remaining. Some of the land at the west end of Ramsbury Road may have been the burial ground for the nunnery. Pieces of gravestones have been found in the gardens.[12]

Sopwell ruins Reproduced from an original Francis Frith postcard held in the collection of St Albans Museum

One famous inhabitant of the nunnery was Dame Juliana Berners, or Barnes, sometimes said to be the prioress, although her name is not on the list of prioresses. It is said that she wrote the *Boke of St Albans* which was first published in 1486 (a later facsimile copy of the book can be seen in the Hatfield Road museum). The first edition covered the subjects of hunting, hawking and heraldry and a later edition included a section on fishing. It is alleged to be the first printed work written in English by a woman and it was one of eight books printed in St Albans. Juliana Berners put Sopwell on the international map and there are many sporting organisations in the USA today which bear her name.

Although it was a sheltered order, many high born ladies stayed there. In 1428 the famous robber captain William Wawe and his band broke into Sopwell expecting to find there a lady of some influence at the royal court. While they were plundering, the hue and cry was raised by a man in the village. This is interesting as it suggests that there was occupation near to the priory. This could have been just outside its gates, or on Sopwell Lane outside the town, or at the top of Green Lane, called Green Lane End (Cottonmill Lane).[13] Another famous guest was said to have been Anne Boleyn, who had to leave court and retire to the country in the height of the scandal concerning her and Henry VIII. She stayed there between 1524 and 1527. It is believed by some historians that Henry VIII subsequently married Anne in the chapel of the Nunnery. However, others says that they married in a chapel at the Peahen Hotel, or it may even have been in Calais or in Blickling Hall, Norfolk![14]

As is well known, the row over Henry's divorce from Catherine in order to marry Anne led to him breaking with the Church in Rome and dispensing with monastic buildings. The last prioress before the Dissolution was Joan Pygot who was paid a pension of £6 per annum.

Around 1534, Richard Lee, later Sir Richard Lee, was appointed bailiff and farmer of the Priory and, following the Dissolution of the Monasteries, the Priory buildings and the land on which they stood were granted to him. The Priory land extended from the original London Road as far as New Barnes Mill. Lee was also granted land around St Julian's Hospital and Eywood, so he probably owned most of what we now know as Sopwell. In 1548, Lee decided to live in St Albans and build a new house over the foundations of the Priory using materials from the Priory and the Abbey buildings. He started building his house in 1550–60. The early form of Tudor houses were in the medieval style so it was probably built around a courtyard, and Lee may even have reused the Nunnery footprint which would have been in that form. The house was called Lee Hall (or Sopwell Hall). Later, in 1562, Lee enclosed his property to form a park and, because it bordered on the highway to London, he had the road diverted. This new road eventually became Old London Road.

When Cottonmill Close was being built, a kiln chamber with five tile-built arches supporting the floor, and stokehole were found. The kiln was probably used for making roof tiles for Sir Richard Lee's house, but it also may have been used to dry lime at a later date. Pottery dating from the sixteenth century was found at the site which suggests it was there at the time of Richard Lee. Nothing is visible now as it was destroyed when the garages were built. Another kiln was found in Mile House Lane. The Mile House seems to be where the corner of Lee's park was, and the kiln was found just outside the park boundary. This was a lime kiln for making mortar probably used for courses of stone for the walls around the park. The early maps show parts of the wall enclosing the park which do appear to be of stone which underlines this theory. A bit of pot was found at this site and, although not conclusive, it could have been mid-sixteenth century.[15]

By this time Lee had given up being a soldier and retired. However in the 1570s, Henry VIII again required his services to build the defences at Berwick and Calais. Having become once more a court favourite, Lee decided that his house should reflect his new status and be rebuilt in the modern Tudor style. So he pulled it down and started to rebuild on the same site. It would have been in an H-shape with two wings and an adjoining wing with a two-storey hall in Tudor style. Unfortunately, Lee died in 1575 before the house was finished. A good description of what the building might have looked like has been preserved on a plan at Gorhambury. The house is shown as a long building with north and south wings, the main block carried through the wings, and ending in gables at east and west. It appears to be of two storeys with an attic, and has a formal garden to the west, and a forecourt with low buildings to the east, in front of which is an outer courtyard entered through the main gateway on the road. To the north of the house is a garden or orchard, and a stream flows close by on the west and south. On the rising ground north of the house is a warren, with a second warren adjoining it, its inhabitants, rabbits and deer, being shown on a colossal scale. To the north-west is a water-mill, marked 'Paper-Mill,' and an inclosure called 'Lawne-Meade,' by the side of the stream, with the warren meadow to the west across the stream, and in front of the house are the 'Litle Lawne' and 'Pond Meade'.[16]

The 'Paper-Mill' is Sopwell Mill.

Lee is buried in St Peter's churchyard. His helmet, which accompanied his coffin, can be seen in St Alban's Museum in Hatfield Road. In his will, he gave Sopwell to his elder daughter Mary (Maud) Coningsby, later Pemberton. Parts of his house were later dismantled and used to restore the manor house in Gorhambury, home of Sir Nicholas Bacon. Some fine plaster medallions of Roman emperors were removed and these can now be seen at Salisbury Hall at Shenley.

The last that is known of Lee Hall being lived in was in 1793 when a Mrs Clark occupied a part of it. The great garden and a garden house were leased in 1706 to William Kilby, a gardener. It then became a ruin. In 1893, Charles Ashdown gives a good description of what the ruins looked like at that time:

> Huge fragments of wall, composed of brick and flint are now the sole remains of this famous Tudor residence. The windows of some of the principal apartments are large and square with stone mullions and many vestiges of ornamentation. Upon a square tablet of stone, placed over a doorway leading into one of the gardens, is a carving in relief (now almost obliterated) of a dexter hand and arm, elevated, and holding a broken sword, this closely resembling the crest granted to Sir Richard Lee; above it is an undecipherable label. A strongly arched brick building, with curious recesses in the sides, stands in one angle of the garden; the thick and massive brick wall, with its buttresses and fragments of alcoves, running by the side of the grounds adjacent to the river, is probably a relic of the Nunnery, and, at the eastern termination of the grounds, the two trout ponds, now overgrown with lilies, may also have the same origin ascribed to them.[17]

The ruins were excavated in 1962–63 by the St Albans and Hertfordshire Architectural and Archaeological Society (SAHAAS). Three floors of Priory churches of various ages were found one on top of the other and laid with tiles. Among the debris, they found painted glass, stonework dating from 1300 and a silver penny from the reign of Henry V. Under the floors were burials and adjacent was a cloister and chapter house.

The boundary walls of Lee's property have 'surfaced' from time to time. In 1890, allotment holders digging in a

> new allotment field near Old London Road and Cotton Mill-lane have experienced trouble in digging during the past few weeks by reasons of masses of solid foundations of walls found. The stone is of Tottenhoe stone and includes four large pieces as well as a well-moulded centre stone of an arch.[18]

When gas pipes were being laid in 1929 in Cottonmill Lane, the workmen found some foundations of a wall two feet below the surface which stretched 12 feet inside the old St Peter's School. The stones appeared to have been hand carved and to have formed the top of the wall. Some of them weighed about half a hundredweight (about 50kg) and were in a good state of preservation, but exposure to the atmosphere had caused others to crack and crumble. The fact that some of the stones were arched suggested that they may have formed part of an underground passage between the convent and the Abbey. However, archaeologists do not believe the theory of a subterranean tunnel on the grounds that it would have to have passed under the river Ver which was at that time of considerable size.[19]

The site in front of the ruins was used as a scrap yard from the late nineteenth century to the first half of the twentieth, and the mound on the right of the ruins near Cottonmill Lane was the site of a motorcycle repair shop. This mound may also have been part of the gatehouse dating from Lee's time. The ruins are now a scheduled national monument.

The Holy Well

Holy Well
2011
© Rick
Taylor

The Holy Well is probably more ancient than any other part of St Albans.[20] It predated the Romans and may well have been pre-Christian. Such holy relics were often Celtic in origin and associated with a feminine deity. Healing is said to take place when a hand or arm is immersed in the water or by throwing in an offering.[21] There is some doubt over whether there was an actual well; it may just have been a spring. Whatever it was, Holywell Hill was named after it. Where it was situated has also been a subject of speculation over the years. It is mentioned on the Andrews and Wren map of Hertfordshire 1766 and in eighteenth century maps, although it is difficult to pinpoint its exact position. In *St Albans Borough Boundary*, Dr Eileen Roberts says that it is not far north-east of the [Holywell] bridge. Nowadays, it is recognised as being just off Holywell Hill in de Tany Court, although this position has never been proved conclusively.

There are many stories and legends surrounding the well's origins and healing properties. The author was taught at school that Alban died on a flowery hill and that his decapitated head rolled down to where a sacred spring mysteriously bubbled. The spring was no doubt already there but maybe it took on sacred properties following Alban's martyrdom. Another version is that, prior to his execution, Alban desired water and a sacred spring bubbled up to quench his thirst. An example given of the efficacy of the water was in a battle fought at St Albans by Uther Pendragon in about 512. Uther was badly wounded, and it was claimed that he was cured by the well water.

According to Matthew Paris in the *Gesta Abbatum Monasterii Sancti Albani*, the Holy Well or spring was the place where the pious ladies who became the nuns of Sopwell Priory dipped their lumps of bread, or sops – hence 'Sopwell' Priory. A well, said to be the Holy Well, was once part of the terraced garden of the Duke and Duchess of Marlborough who built their house, called Holywell House, in the seventeenth century.

> The Holy Well from whence the estate has derived its name is on the lawn adjacent to the garden front and is still held in some estimation for its purity and salubrious qualities.[22]

However, some say that this may have been nothing more than 'an eighteenth century Romantic garden feature'.[23] After Holywell House was demolished in 1825, the land became the playing fields of St Albans School and the well disappeared. Fortunately, some people remembered where it was:

> The Holy Well was situated upon the lawn, and doubtless was well cared for when the house existed; it is now remembered only as a muddy depression, sheltered by the remains of a dilapidated wall and a mournful specimen of a blackthorn; a few years ago since the exigencies of athleticism necessitated the ground being levelled and turfed over, and it is much to be regretted that there is nothing to mark the site of what was essentially one of the most ancient of English 'Holy Wells'.[24]

A Miss Lightfoot, aged eighty-five, who lived on Holywell Hill, wrote a letter to *Hertfordshire Countryside* magazine in 1960 saying:

> I remember the well quite well, for as a child I often went round it. It was surrounded by a fence, inside was a tree, water and weeds – not very inviting.[25]

'Old boys' from St Albans School also recall that in the 1930s there was a concrete slab at one end of their football pitch which they knew as the site of the well.[26] However, after that the well seemed to have been lost.

In the 1980s, the playing field land south of Belmont Hill was set aside for development. There were plans to build a hotel on the site but there was no mention of the well in the plans. This led to many complaints in the local press and suggestions that the well be discovered and preserved. A local dowser claimed to have found the site and a resident whose garden backed onto the site also claimed to have found the well by referring to an old map and the colour of the grass compared to its surroundings.[27] Still nothing was done about it and it looked as if the needs of the commercial developers were paramount. Because of the council's failure to act, some local residents took it upon themselves to organise an unofficial dig. This resulted in some sensational headlines in the local press:

> Holy site desecrated by diggers. Excavation of a historic monument in St Albans has suffered a blow by treasure hunting vandals.

The professional archaeologists were understandably upset:

> Amateur archaeologists searching for the lost Holy Well of St Albans were slammed this week after they uncovered a rubble-filled hole near the supposed site of the well. The excited diggers say the brick-lined pit they found is undoubtedly a late structure over the much older well, which lies under the site scheduled for a hotel and housing. But museum staff at St Albans council say the hole may not be a Holy Well, and have condemned the amateur efforts to find the almost mythical watering place that gave both Holywell Hill and Sopwell their names. The owners of the land said the unofficial dig on Sunday – accompanied by a prominent St Albans lawyer – amounted to trespass.[28]

The hot air circulating amongst professional archaeologists, the museum and the public seemed to wake people up to the fact that the well, once long forgotten, was worth preserving *in situ*. A statement was issued by the council in 1984:

> The council is aware of the public's concern and interest, however the location of the well is

uncertain, and only by excavation can we locate and identify the well to see that it is worthy of preservation. A recent trial excavation failed to positively identify the well. The brick structure recently revealed was found to have been built post 1897, although it caps an earlier structure. This feature is further north than the antiquities cross on the ordnance sheets, and further work and deep excavation will be necessary to seek evidence relating it to the holy well. If conclusive evidence is not found it would be extremely costly, entailing deep excavation over a wide area with no guarantee that a recognisable structure remains. Should the well be in a condition where renovation is possible, whether in its eighteenth century form, perhaps a timber lined structure, the district council's planning brief could insist on retention. If there is no significant trace of the well, a plaque on a nearby building would suffice.

Later, the museum staff did agree to undertake an excavation. They dug a long trench which revealed that there was evidence of an earlier well underneath the modern one – some glass was found which dated back to the Victorian era and some medieval pottery.[29] They also found evidence of a drain leading down to the river and some ancient wooden post holes which could even have been part of a Saxon settlement. The hotel plans were dropped, the well was fenced in and the residential development of de Tany Court was built around it. However, there is still no indication that this really is the Holy Well. An interesting theory is that the well was more likely to have been on the other side of Holywell Hill the east side on the Abbey lands, and as it may have been a pre-Norman holy place, the Norman Abbey suppressed it.[30]

St Stephen's Church

St Stephen's is the oldest church in Sopwell. It stands on the corner of the old Roman road of Watling Street and St Stephens Hill, one of the four churches designed to cover the approach to the town, the others being the Abbey, St Michael's and St Peter's. The original church, built by the Abbot Ulsinus in AD 948, was built on a Roman burial site. This was

St Stephen's
c.1860

replaced in the twelfth century by a Norman construction, parts of which still remain. In 1220 under the then Abbot, William Trumpington, a lady chapel was added. There were no more important changes until 1860, when restoration work was necessary to repair the crumbling church. It boasts the oldest font in St Albans, dated 1350.

St Stephen's must have been in quite an isolated rural setting prior to the twentieth century as this evocative description in the 1890s depicts:

> Delightfully situated upon the summit of one of the loftiest elevations in the vicinity of St Albans, the Parish Church of St Stephen presents a quiet, homely picture of rural peacefulness and rustic simplicity. It is strange, that at such a short distance from the City should be found all the primitive concomitants which generally form the chief characteristics of village life; for here we see the Church (with its rectory) nestling in the trees, the almost deserted street, the village post-office, the inevitable inn occupying the customary position opposite the Church, the dwellings of rich and poor intermingled indiscriminately, while the scent of hay and kine is wafted on the air from the surrounding farmsteads.[31]

Such an idyllic setting is hardly recognisable today.

One of the many items of interest in the church is the brass lectern in the shape of an eagle. The story of how the lectern made its way to St Albans is a fascinating one. The lectern, called the Dunkeld lectern, had been gifted to Scotland by Pope Alexander VI in 1498 and had been taken to Holyrood Abbey where it remained until 1544. The inscription on the orb says: *Georgius Creichton Episcopus Dunkeldensis* – George Creichton Bishop of Dunkeld. He was the abbot at Holyrood from 1515 to 1522 and was probably responsible for presenting the lectern to Holyrood Abbey.[32]

Brass lectern in St Stephen's Church
© Vic Foster

In the sixteenth century, during the reign of Henry VIII, relations between Scotland and England deteriorated. Henry decided to send his army to teach the Scots a lesson and Holyrood Abbey was among the buildings destroyed and plundered by the English army. Sir Richard Lee, Henry's military engineer, was among the destroyers. The Dunkeld lectern was taken from Holyrood Abbey, and as he was later granted the rectorship of St Stephen's as well as Sopwell Nunnery, it was, no doubt, Lee who took it and gave it to Stephen's.

During the English Civil War in the mid seventeenth century, the lectern disappeared. It was found a hundred years or so later in the tomb of the Montague family. It had apparently been put there for safe keeping by the Anglican clergy because the English parliament had passed new laws authorising the destruction of religious images and icons. These were seen as being associated with Catholicism by the Puritans who believed in simple worship.

Meanwhile, the Scottish people – mainly academics and clergy – had become aware of the existence of the lectern and campaigned for its return. Many fruitless approaches were made to the church for it to be restored. In 1972, there was an attempt to steal it and it suffered damage when part of the base was taken. In 1982, it was agreed by the Church of England to loan it to Edinburgh as part of an exhibition of medieval Scottish art. Many patriotic Scots were annoyed when it was returned to St Stephen's, however, and so took the law into their own hands and stole it back in 1984, saying it was being returned to its rightful home. It remained in Scotland after that but was the subject of much heated debate. In 1999 the lectern was delivered to an arts centre on the Royal Mile in Edinburgh, and later, in 2005, a court of the Church of England announced that the lectern, now known as the Holyrood Bird, should be loaned permanently to the National Museum of Scotland. The lectern seen today in St Stephen's Church is, therefore, not the original, but a 150-year-old replica given to the church by the Scottish people in 1995.

One of the most memorable and popular incumbents of St Stephen's Church in recent years was the Revd Anthony Hart-Synnot. He was the vicar of St Stephen's for nearly twenty years before his tragic death, aged fifty-seven, in 1974. He has been described as an eccentric and controversial character who was not afraid to speak his mind – his parish magazine often included controversial topics. Local residents had only good things to say about his generosity and warm-heartedness which sometimes got out of hand as there were some who took advantage of his kindness. He admitted himself that he was a 'mug and a sucker for a hard luck story'. He was also well known for wearing his football boots to services, especially at weddings. When delivering the parish magazine, he was often welcomed in for a drink and a chat. He was also prone to stopping the cars of his parishioners to ask for lifts around the parish and organising collections on the bus.

Kathy Sinfield has memories of Hart-Synnot at the time when she and her husband Jim were trying out their new car:

> Jim had a new car, a metallic beige Renault, and he had just bought it and picked me up from the office and we were at the traffic lights at Chequer Street. Bang, bang on the window, and it was Hart-Synnot and he got in. He said it had a nice smell, and Jim said it was a new car. Hart-Synnot blessed the car. We went out in the evening and went all the way over to Nomansland to the Wicked Lady; we weren't drinkers really, but it was our first drive out. [While we were there] somebody pinched the petrol cap and siphoned all the petrol. Jim said, Don't mention Hart-Synnot!

Pauline Crosier said that he let the troubled teenagers use the rectory which they ruined and so he had to move out. He stayed with whoever would have him. He was in Doggetts Way for a time.

St Stephen's
14.05.1948
© English
Heritage.
NMR Aerofilms
Collection

Joan Forder:

Hart-Synnot was a character. He took a collection on the buses. He never used to pay. He used to go round taking the collection . . . When one of my children was christened, he turned up with all the robes but he had football boots on. When we got married he was the first one up to the bar. It was at the Cottonmill Club I know that. He was very nice but people took advantage of him . . . He took all those mods and rockers in and they stripped the roof of all the lead and pulled the front door off with a rope.

New Barnes House and the Manor of Sopwell[33]

Another famous building in Sopwell is the Sopwell House Hotel. This was originally called New Barnes House and the area around was called New Barnes. It started out as a one-storey Tudor building almost four hundred years ago. The estate of New Barnes was part of the manor of Sopwell and belonged to the Nunnery at Sopwell, a daughter house of the Abbey. In 1534, Sir Richard Lee was described as the bailiff and farmer of the manor of Sopwell, and in 1540 the manor was granted to him. Other manors in the area were Gorhambury, Kingsbury and Windridge.

The estate of New Barnes passed to Maud Coningsby, Lee's daughter. The house was built for her brother-in-law, Sir Ralph Sadleir of Standon Lordship.[34] Sadleir was a military man and also a courtier to the Tudors. As he died in 1587, the house must have been built some time before then. There may have been an earlier, smaller building on the site which was perhaps enlarged and improved for Sir Ralph. Some notes from an architectural survey of the building, made in October 1969 at the time of its development as Sopwell House Hotel, record that:

> [the building] was found to have been built around a timber Tudor building. The main framing timbers of massive size were still in position. The main roof trusses had been cut away to allow a second story to be built on the timber building.

Sopwell estate plan 1666 Courtesy Herts Archive and Library Services

A map of Ayewood (Eywood) in 1600 shows New Barnes House as a two-storied building with two chimneys; a house of respectable size although quite small compared to the representation of Sopwell House (Lee Hall) on the same map. In 1603, as Maud Coningsby had no children, she gave the manor of Sopwell, including New Barnes, to her nephew Richard Sadleir (son of Ralph). The deed is the earliest written reference to a house on the site. It refers to the house as newly built, which could mean perhaps some thirty years previously.[35] It was perhaps a sort of wedding gift, as Richard was married that year to Joyce Honeywood. Richard most probably resided at Lee Hall, as did his son, Robert, who inherited the manor upon Richard's death in 1624.

The New Barnes estate was let to various tenants during the early seventeenth century. The most notable was Alice, Duchess of Dudley, a distant connection of the Lee family, who occupied the house between 1665 and 1667 as a refuge from the Great Plague and the Fire of London. She died in around 1668 at the age of ninety.

After Robert Sadleir's death in 1663 the manor was inherited by his daughter, Helen, and her husband, Thomas Saunders of Beechwood, near Flamstead in Herts. An estate plan of Sopwell in 1666 shows a building very similar to that of 1600. In 1669, Thomas Saunders sold the manor of Sopwell to Sir Harbottle Grimston II, the second baronet. Sir Harbottle had purchased Gorhambury from Henry Meautys in around 1650. Gorhambury was at that time in a very bad state of repair and Sir Harbottle needed money to repair both Gorhambury and Verulam House. He sold much of the manor of Sopwell, presumably at a good profit, and demolished part of Lee Hall, using the materials in his repairs. Some of the stone was used to rebuild Gorhambury Chapel in 1672-3.

The estate at New Barnes was sold to Robert New. The New family were wealthy and very powerful in seventeenth-century St Albans. In his will, dated 1673, Robert New identifies himself as a 'gentleman of New Barnes, St Albans'. His inventory of 1673 shows the house at New Barnes containing:
- two parlours including a 'great parlour' with contents valued at £21;
- four chambers including a 'best chamber' with a French bedstead;
- down bed, silk quilt and wall hangings, valued at £59;
- plate valued at £20 ;
- a brewhouse and mill, valued at £94.

This suggests that, at the time, the mill at New Barnes was part of the property, although at a later date it seems to have been sold separately. Robert left the New Barnes estate entailed to his nephews, the sons of his brother John (who died in 1684). John New had been mayor of St Albans in 1659, 1670 and 1682. John's eldest son, William, had died before his uncle, so the estate was inherited by his second son, another John. It is probable that he did not live there but let the estate of New Barnes to a Thomas Robins(on), a yeoman as it was Robins(on) who paid the poor rates at New Barnes between at least 1675 and 1680. When John died in 1702, the estate became the property of his eldest son, Robert (II) (1673-1708).

Robert New (II) in his will describes himself as a 'Gentleman of Gray's Inn and New Barns' [sic]. His will was written in 1703 shortly after he inherited the property, which indicates that his health could not have been good. He married Elizabeth Strong, the daughter of Edward Strong. In his will he left New Barnes to Elizabeth for her lifetime and, after her death, to his only son Robert (III) (1700-1762). However, between 1703 and 1708 Robert and Elizabeth had three more sons, the last, Thomas, was born shortly before his father's death in 1708. Thomas died unmarried in 1736. Edward married and had two daughters, and John married but died without issue. Robert (II) died in 1708. Between 1708 and 1714, his widow, Elizabeth, sold the estate to her father Edward Strong, probably with a condition that it would be left to her eldest son, Robert (III), as her husband had desired, and this is what happened.

Edward Strong is usually referred to as 'the master mason' and he was descended from a long line of masons. He was famous for having founded the Freemasons and was a close friend of Sir Christopher Wren. Strong resided at New Barnes from the time he purchased it until his death in 1723. He probably made the alterations to the house which appear in the Oldfield drawing of c. 1800 which shows

> a house of 18th century appearance, partly of three storeys and five bays and partly of two storeys and two bays; the front doorway is off-centre, being in the end bay of the taller part next to the lower part, so that it can be interpreted in the light of Salisbury Hall, Shenley, as the rebuilding in two phases of the late sixteenth century house … [he] may have been responsible for the five-bay part.[36]

Edward Strong left New Barnes to his grandson Robert New III (1700-1762) in 1723. New became a solicitor at the Middle Temple. Although he lived in London during the law terms, his will refers to various household goods, paintings, silver and china at New Barnes, so it was also occupied by him as his country home. His wife, Frances (Glanville), died in 1758, and he may have spent more of his later life in his home in Shire Lane in London. (The Sopwell House Hotel brochure states that the house was occupied in 1754 by the Verulam family, but no authority is given.)

A childless widower, Robert left New Barnes to his brother John New for his lifetime and after John's death to his two nieces (daughters of his brother Edward), Elizabeth Halifax and Margaret New. John New died in 1772. In 1799, the estate of New Barnes was sold to Matthew Towgood. On 10th January 1799, he paid 6s and 8d land-tax as proprietor. He and his wife, Margaret, may have rented it to start with as their daughter Jane 'of New Barnes' was baptised in 1798 at St Albans Abbey. A tenth child, Ann, was born at New Barnes in 1800. In 1802 Margaret died and, two years later, Matthew married Ann Gibson of Somerset. They had three children while at New Barnes. In 1810 Matthew sold the estate to Joseph Timperon.

Matthew Towgood's big contribution to the estate was a redesign of the park and garden. In 1802, he hired Humphrey Repton, the famous landscape designer who was then at the peak of his career. Unfortunately, no (contemporary) evidence for the implementation of the plans described in Repton's Red Book of notes for the project exists, until we read it in the 1886 sale particulars for the property. His proposals dealt with the views to the south-east and south-west and the approach and view to the north. A line of trees and a hedge obstructed the views to the south-east and south-west and a straight canal above ground-level was the nearest water. Repton proposed making openings in the line of trees and the hedge and replacing the canal with a water-course slightly below ground-level, curving toward the house. This would have created a smaller garden which was devoted to flowers and shrubs. The canal was replaced instead by a curving fishpond at ground-level rather further away, so creating a larger garden. To the north, he recommended that a copse be planted around the bend in Cottonmill Lane to hide the lane from view and that the field be planted with some trees to give a park-like appearance with an approach through the park. The planting was done, but Towgood objected to the approach through the park because it showed visitors the most beautiful part of the estate. An entrance with an arch and two lodges was built at the bend instead. This is now Sopwell Gate Lodge. Repton did not find this sort of entrance pleasing, but he did often build them, and so these may have been designed by Repton (or his son). In 1822 Repton was hired by the next owner, Joseph Timperon, but his notes for this project have not survived. Some of the above work may have been done at this time, but no map of the estate between 1802 and 1886 exists.

Timperon, born in Cumberland in 1762, purchased the estate in 1810. He was a very wealthy merchant who made a fortune in the West Indies. He married Anne Kyte in London

in 1806 and they had seven children, three of whom predeceased him. The Jamaican properties, as well as those he owned in England and all his business and all his investments, were inherited by his sons John Robert and Arthur Matthias upon his death in 1846. His will, written in 1843, instructed his sons and his trustees to sell the Jamaican properties. He may have been aware of coming events, because in 1846 the government passed a law to equalise the tariff on sugar which led to the collapse of the sugar industry in the West Indies. John Robert Timperon died in 1848 and, after Arthur Matthias Timperon's death in 1855, the vast estate was inherited by Joseph's youngest daughter, Isabella Charlotte Worley. She was the last of the family. Her husband, Henry Thomas Worley, died in 1855. They had no children. Isabella Worley used the great wealth she inherited in many acts of generosity to the people of St Albans. Her last act of kindness was to provide tea and cakes for the Christmas party at St Peter's School in 1882. She died in 1883. The estate was sold by her trustees in 1886 and the house and its grounds were bought by the Earl of Verulam (the Grimston family). The house at this time is described in the sale particulars:

New Barnes is bounded by the River Ver on the West, a tributary of the Colne, and in many parts equally celebrated for its fishing; advantage has been taken of the river to form a Small Lake divided into upper and lower portions, which afford an agreeable diversification of Scenery close to the Residence. The West side of the Stream is a part of the Gorhambury Estate of the Rt. Hon. the Earl of Verulam. The Mansion is approached from the High Road through a Stone Arched Gateway with Lodge Entrance, through the Park and so by a Carriage Drive to the Front door . . . There is an Entrance Way, paved with coloured Stone Squares, and a hall of the same. On the right is The Dining room with Alcove, with coloured marble mantle and good grate. On the Left is The Library with deep moulded long Marble Mantel. Beyond there is The Drawing Room, with valuable Carved White Marble Mantel. A lift-up window and Verandah lead to the Flower Garden. The upper part of the House is approached by three Staircases. On the first floor The Oak room with Pretty Alcove used as a sitting room or boudoir also [three bedrooms, two with dressing rooms, and three other rooms]. Above this is the second floor containing six large and two small bedrooms, a store room. On the ground floor are the Offices comprising a gun room, butler's pantry, servants' hall, a well-fitted kitchen . . . larder, housekeeper's room, sculery, and under the house, excellent wine cellars . . . There are three W. C.'s, one of which is in the Top Storey and two on the Ground Floor. A beautiful Conservatory communicating with the House, about 34 feet long, with tessellated Floor and artificially heated, is on the South side of the House and forms a pleasant and elegant adjunct.

The Grimston family resided there for some years, probably from shortly after the sale in 1886 until spring 1901. They may have been letting Gorhambury to raise funds for its upkeep. New Barnes was leased in 1901 by Prince Louis of Battenberg as a country home for his family. Prince Louis was the father of Louis, later Lord Mountbatten of Burma, and his daughter, Alice, married Prince Andrew of Greece and became the mother of Prince Philip, Duke of Edinburgh. It is believed that Prince Andrew proposed to Alice in the gardens at Sopwell House.

In 1891, the estate was referred to as Sopwell Park. There was a coachman living in the Coachman's House, Sopwell Park, and there was also a laundress whose address was Sopwell Laundry, Sopwell Park. In 1907 New Barnes 'called also Sopwell House' is described in the *Victoria County History of Hertfordshire* as 'a large brick house, plastered and painted, with extensive grounds, the greater part of which is occupied by the Verulam Golf Club'. This is the first mention of the name Sopwell House for the property. At this time Mr A.T. Buller was renting the estate.

During the twentieth century, the house was occupied by various members of the Grimston family until the end of the Second World War when it became a home for the aged, by which time it was described as old and decaying. Visitors in 1967 described the conditions for the elderly inmates as bleak and Dickensian.[37] The vast hall contained no floor covering, just bare boards with wooden trestle tables arranged in a row down the middle of the huge room. There were decrepit chairs, many of which had their horsehair stuffing coming out of them, placed round the room where the old people would sit staring into space. The house was closed soon after and converted in 1969 into a hotel by the Newling-Wards. The present owner, Abraham Bejerano, purchased the property from the Newling-Ward family in 1986. It is now one of the more prestigious hotels in the country and is popular with the many famous football teams who stay there.

Mrs Terry, who lived in Sopwell Gate Lodge in the 1930s, remembers one of the New Barnes House tenants: Major Barnett and his family.

Lady Barnett and Major Barnett lived in the house. She was always getting pulled over for speeding. Although they had a chauffeur, she liked to do it herself and was always getting into trouble with the police over the driving. The son, Cedric, we will always remember him because he used to come into this field opposite to where we lived with a boomerang. He used to throw it. Whether it came back to him I don't know!

Bill Mackenzie also has some memories of Sopwell Gate Lodge:

Where they built that new house up the road there, that was the original gatehouse. Because if you go where the original gatehouse is, there's a little footpath around the back that the golfers use to cross the road. There was a tee up there, and if you stand up there and look across that field you can see where a different bit of grass is growing – you can see a different coloured grass coming from the Lodge gate. If you stand on the tee on the golf course and look across where the grass is a foot high, it's a different colour as it must have a different base underneath it. You can see the sweep where the drive used to go through them little houses – there used to be two families living there. The right-hand one used to be just one big room and there was a family there called Duffy – there was a mother and father and three sons all living in that one room. On the left-hand side there was a family called Lucas: a father and daughter and a son lived in that. That was it, there was no house at the back.

Some residents remember a mysterious brick-built structure in the grounds of New Barnes House near the Lodge. Was it a cesspit, a secret tunnel to the Abbey or an ice-house?

Betty Terry:

When we lived in the Lodge, there was no light or heating or anything. We had oil lamps and no loo except one outside, and it had no chain or anything and my poor father had to go to a spinney there. Now, there was a brick built gadget, and everybody said it was either a tunnel going to the Abbey or to the Nunnery. My father said it wasn't; it was just a cesspit. It was a brick building covering this big hole. Well, my poor father had to carry the buckets from the toilet into the spinney and the rubbish [to put] into the cesspit.

Bill Mackenzie:

There was a little copse of trees at the back of that house, and it always fascinated me because you go in there and there was a brick archway and you can only go in about six or seven foot when there was a drop. We never got the courage to go down. We never did know what it was for. We just assumed it was something to do with Sopwell House – a cold store for them or something like that. The kids used to say that it was a secret passage going all the way to the Abbey!

Kathy Sinfield:

Sopwell House was there but it was very dilapidated. I don't know if it was inhabited then or whether there was a nursing home or something there. But the gateway which is still standing in the now existing Cottonmill Lane going out to London Road past Sopwell House had an ice-house which was of course dug into the ground. I don't know if it still exists. You can't see it now because of the houses – accommodation for the staff I think. There was this ice-house where they used to keep the ice.

Vic Foster also remembers the ice-house being halfway between the Lodge and the House and it had bones in it. He said it had a dome shape underground with an entrance in an embankment leading to a short, rounded tunnel and then to a large brick-lined pit.

Peter Smith, Senior Planning Officer, Conservation and Design, from St Albans District Council, said that they did not have any information about an ice-house in the grounds of New Barnes House although most country houses of that size would probably have had one. He also said that there were no signs in the immediate grounds to the south. On the 1880 OS map, there was a small circle marked in a circular spinney close to the gate lodge but it was not present on the 1900 map. Aerial photos show that this spinney still exists with mature trees, so traces may still survive.

There is a record in the Hertfordshire Sites and Monuments database which is based on a letter sent to the *Herts Advertiser* in 1984. This says there was a bowl-shaped brick ice-house in a small wood that now lies within Verulam golf course. It was still used in the twentieth century to supply Sopwell House. It was described as having a short tunnel with a wooden door at the entrance, and the ice stored in it was cut from 'Wirley's Pond across the way'. A subsequent site visit in May 1999 found no traces of the structure. The whereabouts of Wirley's pond is not known. Mrs Terry confirmed that this description matched what she remembered. On a visit to the golf course in 2011, the spinney was easily identified. There is a big pit there covered in trees and vegetation which suggests it may have been where the ice-house was. Also, two concrete slabs were found near the top which may have come from the structure.

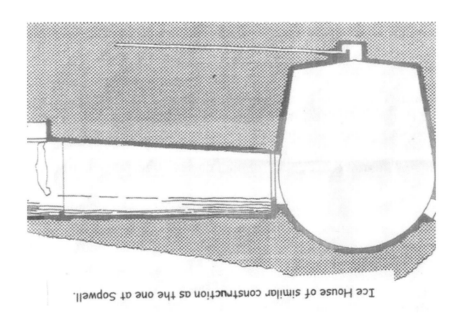

Ice House of similar construction as the one at Sopwell.

Sopwell House Hotel is now a Grade II listed building. The small group of buildings adjacent to Sopwell House and New Barnes Mill was designated as a conservation area in 1973. The two residential properties, Dhobi Lodge and Laundry Cottage, are late Victorian estate cottages. There is another group of buildings which were once part of Sopwell Home Farm. These, including the farm house, have been converted into further accommodation for the hotel. Opposite the mill is a substantial weather-boarded barn of seventeenth century origin now in use by Blacks of Sopwell, formerly Tony's Pine. However, it is believed by the Black family that this barn did not originate in Sopwell but was moved from elsewhere.

Holywell House

Holywell House, the birthplace and home of Sarah Jennings who became the Duchess of Marlborough, has a long history. The original house was situated at the bottom of Holywell Hill and occupied the site of the present waterworks. The house must have been built by the sixteenth century as Elizabeth I stayed there when she was still only a princess. It was owned at the time by Sir Ralph Rowlatt. He died childless so it passed down to his sister who married into the Jennings family. The Jennings family also owned Water End in Sandridge.

Sarah Jennings was born in 1660 in Holywell House. She went to court when she was thirteen and became a favourite of Queen Anne. It was there she met her future husband John Churchill. He was made Duke of Marlborough in the reign of William and Mary. When they were married they came to live in Holywell House which was given to Sarah as part of her dowry, and it was said to be her favourite residence.

The Churchills had a lot of influence at court and became very rich. Towards the end of the seventeenth century they decided to demolish the old Holywell House, as well as many other smaller properties on either side of Holywell Hill, and build a house to match their elevated status. They also extended their lands to include the route of Holywell Hill and had the road diverted to run around the back of their estate. The traffic up and down the hill had to take this new winding route which was later to become Grove Road. The new house would have been a little further uphill from the previous one, nearer Belmont Hill. They had a wonderful landscaped garden which stretched down to the river, which had also been diverted to suit the landscaping. A sales document from 1814 described it as a:

Substantial and well built house with extensive pleasure grounds having lawns, plantations, open and shady walks and shrubberies, a conservatory, rustic temples, spacious fishponds, an orchid farm and stables.[38]

It also had a large orchard, a kitchen garden and pastures for horses and cattle. The Holy Well was also in their garden. The largest fishpond was a long rectangular canalised part of the river, and its remaining earthworks are probably in the fenced-off area of Pocket Park near the entrance to de 'Tany Court and Albeny Gate.[39] Pocket Park is the current name for the green space between Holywell Hill and Cottonmill Lane which follows the course of the river. The Duke was said to like fishing for trout from his fishponds.

The Duke and Duchess were delighted with their new home. Even after building Blenheim Palace several years later, Sarah said she still preferred Holywell House. She described it as 'A clean, sweet house and gardens, tho' ever so small.' There is a plaque on the north corner of Belmont Hill which describes Holywell House as being their favourite. In 1837, the house was demolished in order to allow the turnpike down Holywell Hill to be widened and straightened.

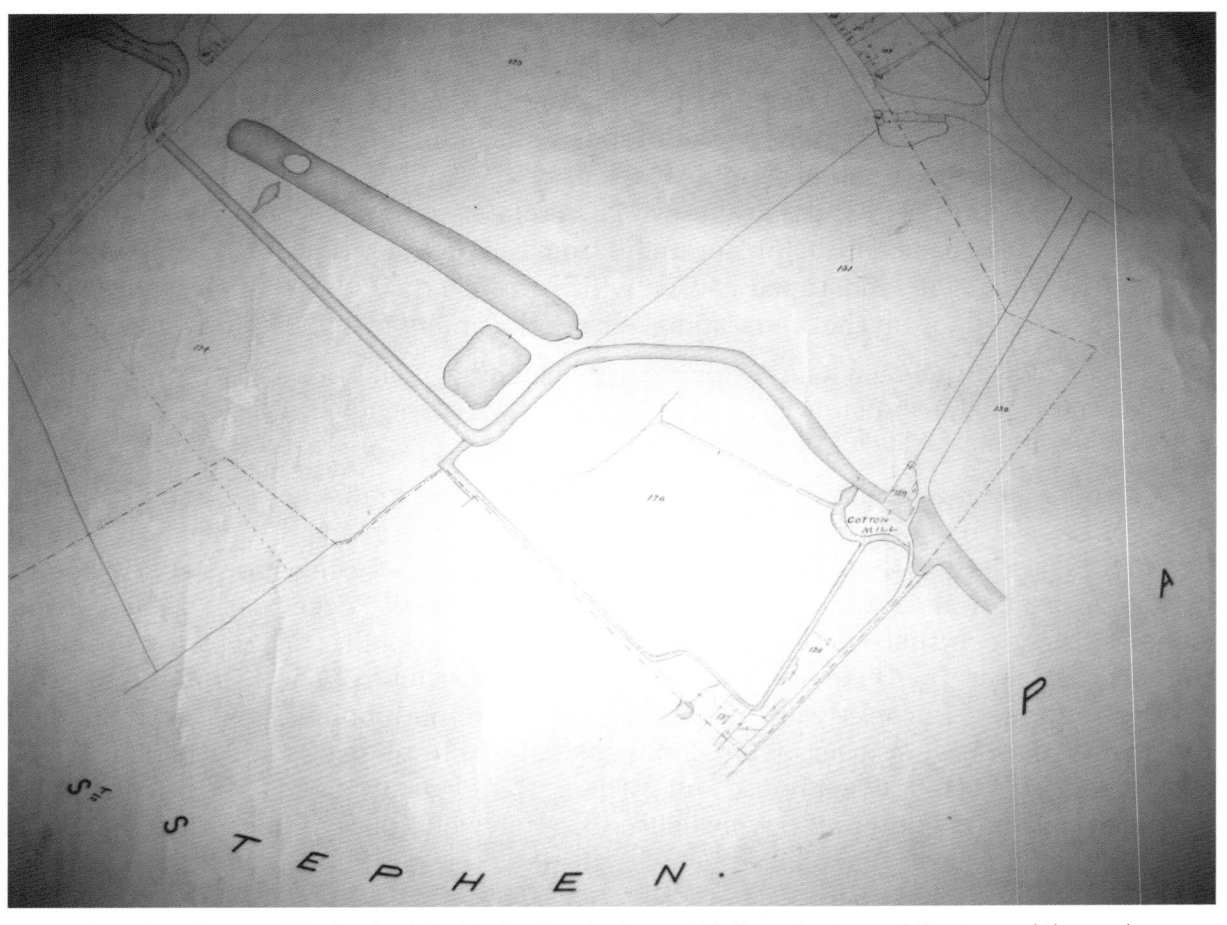

Extract from the tithe map of St Stephen's Parish showing the Cotton Mill. Note the shape of the river and the ponds
Courtesy Herts Archive and Library Service

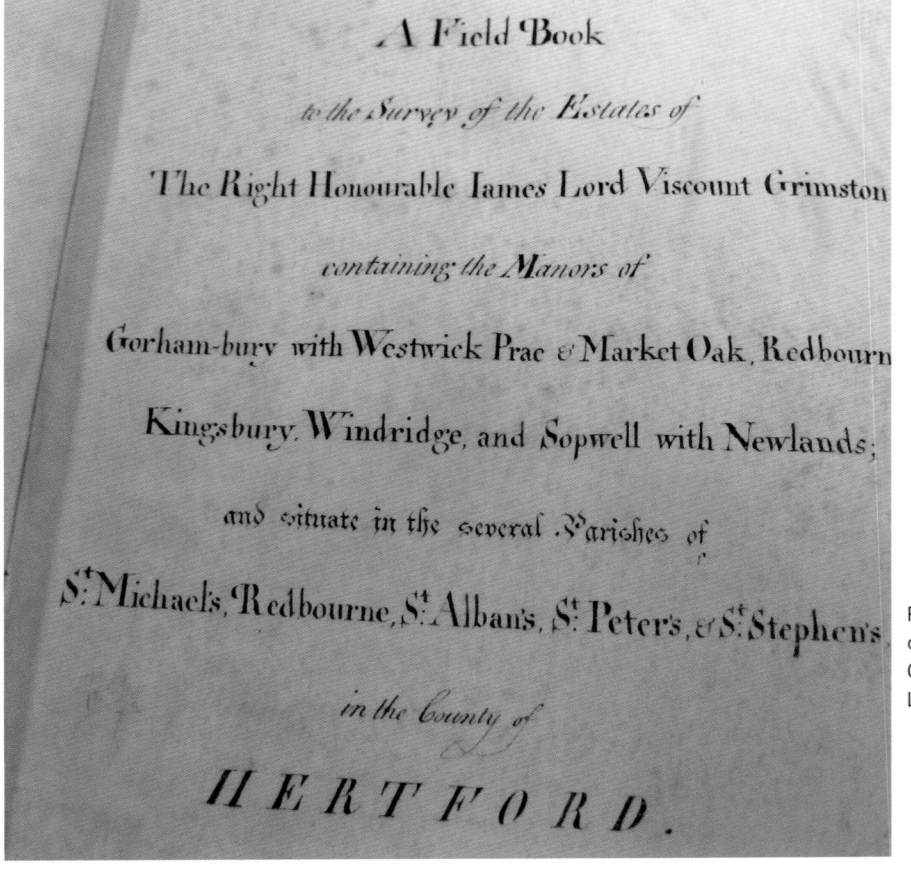

Field Book showing the manor of Sopwell 1766-7
Courtesy Herts Archive and Library Service

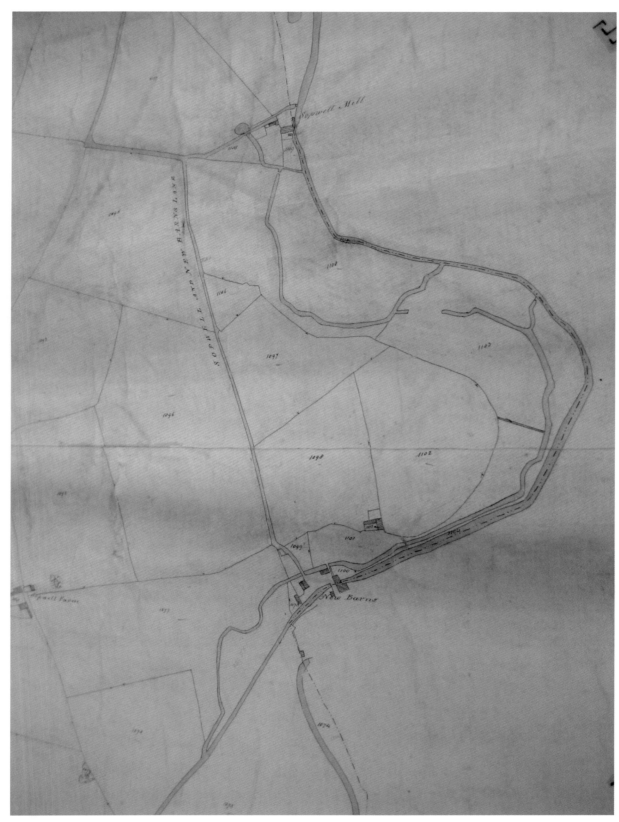

Tithe map from 1847
Note the road from Sopwell Mill to new Barnes Mill is called 'Sopwell and new Barnes Lane'
Courtesy Herts Archive and Library Service

Sopwell Mill
© Mark Boxer

Chapter Two
Rural industries

Practically all of the Sopwell area was covered in fields and farmland until fairly recently. Residents are fortunate to have many of those green spaces around which continue to give Sopwell a rural atmosphere. Most of the farms have disappeared although there is still plenty of farmland remaining as well as some of the old buildings. All the farms were part of the Manor of Sopwell and leased to tenant farmers and millers. It is not certain whether much grain was grown and harvested. Being in the Ver valley, much of the land was probably unsuitable for cereal crops. A lot of it was grassland for making hay. The farms mentioned below often appear to change their names which can be confusing. For example: Sopwell Farm may have been the one at New Barnes, Sopwell Mill, part of Hedges Farm or even the farm at the Nunnery!

There were also mills dating back to before the Dissolution of the Monasteries, and the river and the availability of natural springs gave rise to the watercress industry in the nineteenth century.

In the eighteenth century Sopwell Manor had two corn mills and a paper mill, all three powered by water. The milling of grain into flour was essential to daily life and became one of the reasons, at least in St Albans, for the Peasants' Revolt in 1381. Before the Dissolution of the Monasteries, the land all around St Albans was owned by St Albans Abbey. In the fourteenth century, the Abbot, a very unpopular man who sided with the ruling elite, imposed punishments for private hand-milling, so forcing the people to pay to use the Abbey mills. He actually took possession of the millstones. This incurred the wrath of the peasants who protested. One of the leaders was a William Grindcobbe who led peasants into the Abbey and smashed the stones to pieces.[40] After the Dissolution, the mills were granted, along with the land, to Sir Richard Lee and passed down through the generations.

The Cotton Mill

On or near the site of the swimming baths in Cottonmill Lane there was an actual cotton mill. There are no physical traces left of the mill today but there are literary references to give us clues about the activity there and what it was like. It was an important mill from the late eighteenth to late nineteenth century and was used for the spinning and weaving of cotton. However, it is thought to have had many other uses. Before 1768, it was known as 'the water house' and was the source of domestic water supply to the town.[41] It is shown on the Dury and Andrews large scale map of St Albans of 1766, where it is called the 'Water Works' and was the property of the Corporation of St Albans. It was also being used in the late eighteenth century for polishing diamonds. By the early nineteenth century the mill was making cotton wicks for candles and, later, Berlin wool for tapestry and needlework. In the 1840s, over sixty people worked in this mill.[42] Flour was also milled here. By the 1870s, it was no longer a working mill and it was pulled down shortly after.[43]

In the late 1790s, George Gill lived and worked there. He is listed as the only cotton manufacturer in St Albans.[44] In 1823, William Harris is listed as a cotton spinner; in 1828/9, William Harris and John Staples are listed as cotton spinners; and in 1839, Henry Dupree is listed as a candle wick manufacturer at St Albans Cotton Mill.[45] William Harris and his

Cotton mill
Artist
unknown

step-son-in-law, Edward Jeanneret, were partners in the cotton business. The business folded in 1835 and was presumably taken over by Dupree.

The Cotton Mill also appears to have been something of an early religious community centre. In 1794, the occupants, George Gill and Samuel Maxey, allowed a congregation of Nonconformists to use the mill as a chapel. A Sunday school was even started there to instruct the children of St Albans in the doctrine of the Christian religion.[46] The congregation did not stay long, however, as the premises were seen to be too small for their purpose and they moved to a building off Sweet Briar Lane (now Victoria Street). In 1822, the mill was again registered as a meeting place for an independent congregation and, as late as 1844, one of its rooms was similarly registered as a meeting place for 'Protestant Dissenters'.[47]

It is interesting to note that at one time the borough boundary passed through the Cotton Mill, and in 1804 there is a record of the mayor and aldermen and various other officials 'perambulating the boundaries' – or 'Beating the Bounds' as it is called today – and passing the mace through the Cotton Mill. This was followed by the mayor exercising the manorial right of fishery by fishing in the river.[48]

What did the mill look like? An early engraving indicates that there were two or three buildings with tiled roofs and a square tower with 'sails like a windmill', in the centre. It also had a balcony round the tower.[49] Oldfield also sketched the mill and there is a painting by J.H. Buckingham which can be seen in the St Albans Museum collection.

Sopwell Mill Farm

In Cottonmill Lane, almost opposite Priory Walk, there is a little track which leads down to Sopwell Mill Farm. The original mill on this site was probably one of the three St Albans mills referred to in the Domesday Book. There was certainly a mill here at the time of the Peasants' Revolt in 1381. In the sixteenth and seventeenth centuries, it was a paper mill. Paper in those days was made by pulping linen and cotton rags in water and the watermill was used to power the machinery. The mill was rebuilt in 1691 as a corn mill and stayed in productive use until 1931.

The present mill is predominantly late Victorian. The previous mill was destroyed by fire in 1883. The mill was rebuilt in 1890 although milling appeared to carry on without a break.[50] The present tenants say that one of the farm barns shows evidence of the fire damage.

From census records and wills it has been possible to establish the names of some of the tenants. In the late eighteenth century, the miller was Henry Norris who died in 1783.[51] In 1811, the farmer and miller was also Henry Norris, presumably his son. He was succeeded by Samuel Smith.[52] In the 1841 census, Samuel Smith was still the miller assisted by his son Frederick. In 1851, George Lawrence was a journeyman miller, although he did not live at the mill. He lived at Sportsman's Hall in

Sopwell Mill before the fire of 1883 Courtesy Margaret Wickens

Cottonmill Lane and the mill was occupied by an agricultural labourer called Abraham Long. In 1861, the mill was occupied by the Climance family. Alfred Climance was described as a miller employing one man. In the 1871 and 1881 census, Edmund Hinton and his wife Betsy lived there – his occupation was described as a miller and farmer of 20 acres employing one man. It was in his time that the mill caught fire and was destroyed. (See Appendix 4 for the detailed description given in the *Herts Advertiser.*)

The next tenant is one of its more famous millers: George Butterfield. His address in the 1891 census was Sopwell Mill, Sopwell Park. George Butterfield was a master miller, who came with his family to Sopwell Mill Farm probably in 1884. According to his great-granddaughter, Margaret Wickens, he and his six siblings were born in Chesham Bois between 1833 and 1856 and it was there that he became a miller. For a short time, he took over the mill in Wendover (a sail mill) on the understanding that there was to be an additional watermill when the Wendover Branch Canal was built.[53] However, the building of the canal was delayed, so he decided to leave and take over Sopwell Mill in St Albans. His granddaughter, Grace (Butterfield) Fitzjohn, who was born at the mill in 1896, maintained that he came to rebuild the mill after the fire in 1883 which completely destroyed it. Records show that George and his wife had six children: four born in Chesham Bois, one in Wendover and the last one in St Albans in 1885. The farm, which had commodious barns and outbuildings for cattle and pigs, was run by George's brother, Thomas. The family traded in both grain and dairy products. George's wife, Eliza, was said to be an extremely thrifty person who managed the finances of both the mill and the farm.

George Butterfield junior at Sopwell Mill Courtesy Margaret Wickens

Unfortunately, George Butterfield's milling days were cut short. In 1907 he had a terrible accident. It was a very cold winter and he went outside to chip the ice of the waterwheel and was struck on the head by a falling icicle. As a result of his injuries, he lost his sight and hearing and was never able to work again. His son, also called George, took over the running of the business. George (senior) was looked after by his family at the mill until his death in 1927. Grace (Butterfield) Fitzjohn, writing in 1987, recalls:

> I have a vivid memory of when there was heavy rain, the men folk would get up at all hours during the night to set the water wheel in motion and start all the machinery going (which was all made of wood) in order to use the river water and prevent it overflowing the bank.

George (junior) also had a family business in Albert Street. His granddaughter, Margaret Wickens, said that he was quite a character and very strong:

> Although being very short, he could carry a hundredweight of corn on each shoulder. I am told that when they moved from Wendover to St Albans when he was fourteen years old, he cycled behind the removal van on his penny-farthing bike. He played cricket for a local side and played the piccolo in the town band. Even when he was in his seventies, he was still active and rode a drop handlebar bicycle replacing his penny-farthing. He also kept an allotment. Later the cricket was replaced by bowls. He liked his daily pint and dominoes at the local pub.

For the first half of the Butterfield family's tenure, flour continued to be milled for human consumption but later, competition from larger mills meant that small-scale family operations were producing solely for animal feed. Margaret Wickens says:

> After the 1914–18 war, there was a decline in the flour milling industry in general and many mills were closing down. After my great grandfather died in 1927, the shop in Albert Street was sold and my grandparents and the unmarried girls moved into the mill. Financial problems were increasing.

By 1931, the mill was no longer profitable. Demand for animal feed was decreasing and the mill was owed £440 and 14 shillings in unpaid bills, so after forty-seven years of tenancy, the family decided to relinquish their lease and realise their farm assets. The sale of the stock, mill and farm equipment took place on 7th September 1931. Included in the sale were ten good dairy cows, eleven in-calf Shorthorn heifers (in grand condition), a Roan Shorthorn bull, two horses, a Saddleback sow and twelve pigs. There were 125 items listed in the sale catalogue. With their departure in 1931, all milling ceased in St Albans. George bought two houses in Ramsbury Road (numbers 50 and 52), living with his wife and youngest daughter in one and renting out the other.

The next tenant for the mill and farm was Frederick Coaker. Betty Cutler, who lives on the corner of the lane to the farm, recalls that he was

> A crusty old man and he used to have a pony and trap and take his milk in a churn and he had a daughter. You never used to see him very often. They were isolated down there.

Margaret Brown also remembers Mr Coaker coming round with his horse and cart to deliver milk. Gerry Dunham says that when he died, his daughter delivered the milk on a motorbike with a sidecar. Milk bottles with the name Coaker on them have been found at the mill.

In 1943, the mill was leased to the Blower family: a mother with two unmarried daughters, Dawn and Gig. After Mrs Blower died, the two spinster sisters kept the farm there until 1993. Many local residents remember the two Misses Blower who stabled horses and kept kennels. They also had a pet shop in London Road. Gerry Dunham says they also kept mice.

Betty Cutler remembers the Blowers:

Old milk bottles found at Sopwell Mill farm
© Sandy Norman

I remember it as a farm and then the Misses Blowers took it on and they had dogs, the kennels –boarding kennels. I remember her coming up the lane on a horse in all her riding gear, Dawn Blower . . . I don't know why but my brother always used to buy them a Christmas present. We used to make sloe gin and my brother bought this decanter and strained the sloe gin in it and gave it to them and they were over the moon! They always brought us up a dressed chicken, because we didn't have chicken every day then!

Bill Mackenzie:

They lost a dog one day and there was me and two or three mates went down to help them look for it. They found it under the wheel, it had fallen in the wheel . . . I never actually saw the wheel turning but there was a sluice gate just before you get to it. They used to open that and the water came down to the field and went under another little bridge – because the river Ver comes down and the water would come round . . . and it wanders through the golf course. I suppose in case it flooded or they didn't want to use the wheel or something.

Pauline Crosier remembers that Blower's Farm had a narrow track and that she and her friends used to climb trees down there.

Vic Foster remembers that there was a pond in the field next to the farm which contained hundreds of newts. A willow tree overhung the pond that children used to climb. The pond was filled in when the field became a playing field.

Sopwell Mill Farm became a private house when the two Blower sisters left in 1993. The mill pond is still there and the external mill wheel, now looking extremely worse for wear, is described as cast iron, fourteen feet in diameter and five feet six inches wide (excluding paddles).[54] One of the cogs from the mill machinery was given to Redbournbury mill during its restoration.

A relatively modern description of Sopwell Mill Farm found in an advertisement for rent says:

Sopwell Mill Farm . . . tucked away off Cottonmill Lane the small, riverbank farmhouse and large mill buildings come with two acres of water meadow, looseboxes, a byre, piggeries and an optional sixteen acres of extra land.[55]

New Barnes mill and farm

New Barnes Mill, at the bottom of Cottonmill Lane, stands near to the Sopwell House Hotel and was a flour mill. It was sometimes called Sopwell Mill which must have been very confusing. There is thought to have been a mill on this site since at least the seventeenth century.[56] It was rebuilt in the 1890s by the Earl of Verulam, whose son, Lord Grimston, was living on the estate at Sopwell (New Barnes) House. The buildings have been extended as recently as the 1990s.

The British Flour Research Committee ran the mill from the 1920s and then, in the 1930s, it was operated by the Co-operative Wholesale Society and then Whitworth Brothers until 1957. The present buildings are now used for light industry and business.

In the late eighteenth century, John and Mary Parrott worked the mill and farmed the surrounding land.[57] The census records reveal that living at New Barnes Mill in 1851 was a William Smith, the miller, and his family; Elizabeth Cook, a dairymaid; William Crockett and Joseph Pickett, ploughmen; and some farm boys. The ploughmen and farm boys probably worked on the nearby farm. By 1911, there are no millers listed, only flour workers. John Rudd was described as a flour worker at New Barnes Mill living at Elm Cottage. A Charles Holding, living at Mill Cottage, was also a flour mill worker.

Betty Terry, who lived at Sopwell Gate Lodge in the 1930s, remembers the mill lorries which transported the wheat to Silvertown in London where there was a huge flour mill:

One day we were playing in these sheds which were all stacked up with the wheat and we got told off dreadfully because we could have had a bad accident. The mill lorries used to come back and forth all the time. One day the lorry drivers said they would take my brother – he was very tiny at the time – to Silvertown and I cried my eyes out because they wouldn't take me, because they couldn't take a girl. They were in Silvertown for the day and they thoroughly enjoyed it. They used to go up there to unload the flour or wheat. Mill lorries were always around. I had a little cat at the time called Minnie and they ran over it and it got killed.

Alfie Francis worked there but gave the job up as he didn't like the all the flour dust. Kathy Sinfield remembers the mill as a working mill when they were getting the corn in.

The big concrete thing outside used to be covered in flour.

The farm at New Barnes has had several names over the years. The most recent name is Sopwell Home Farm as the area around was called Sopwell Park, or just Sopwell. All the fields adjacent to the river were part of the farm and all the buildings near the river, apart from the mill, were farm buildings and cottages. Many of the original farm buildings are now part of the Sopwell House Hotel or are used as business premises.

David Snoxall was an agricultural labourer, and his wife, a laundress in the census of 1851. His address was New Barns (*sic*). In 1871 and 1881 the farm bailiff was an Alexander Innes who came from Scotland. There are buildings nearby called Laundry Cottages, and many of the farm workers' wives were laundresses. This suggests that the cottages were once used for doing the washing for the big house at New Barnes. Laundry Cottage and Dhobi Lodge still exist today. 'Dhobi' also means laundry.

Field at Brown's (Sopwell Home) Farm in 1930s © Betty Terry

Betty Terry's father, Mr Giddings, worked at this farm in the late 1920s to early 1930s. She called it Brown's Farm as Mr Brown was then the farmer. William Brown appears as a dairy farmer in Kelly's directory in 1932. Mr Giddings worked as a cowman and the family lived at Sopwell Gate Lodge:

Dad was the cowman and there was a gentleman called Miles and he was a horseman and his son was in the *Herts Advertiser* some years ago because he was the last horse and cart man to drive through the town, Freddy his name was . . . Some time after we'd been there, Mr Brown wanted my mother to do the milk, sterilise it or whatever they do with it. The room was cold and damp and he wanted her to stay there and work and she had three young children to get ready for school in the mornings so she just could not cope so they had a row – my dad and Mr

Brown – over it and he got the sack, because the house went with the job so we were homeless really. The only thing I remember about my dad was one year he had to go to Smithfield and show a cow and it was called Blackton Magnet. I don't know how I remember this but they called it Maggie. It didn't win a prize . . .

Margaret Wickens used to go mushrooming in Brown's meadow which she said was the field on the right-hand side of the bridge going from Cottonmill to the Mile House. Margaret Brown remembers cows in the water meadows by the river and that she got chased once. Bobby Jones says that, up until about 1980, she bought turkeys from the farm at Christmas. Nancy Broadbent also remembers buying vegetables at the weekend from the farm.

Little Sopwell Farm

There was another farm called Little Sopwell Farm which is marked on OS maps in the 1930s. There is no farm there now. On the map, the farm buildings were situated to the east of St Julians Hill (Watling Street) near the Watford railway track, halfway between St Julians Hill and New Barnes Mill and right on the borough boundary. In earlier OS maps the name Sopwell Barnes appears in the same area so this is probably a previous name for this farm. The name Barnes suggests farm buildings and, according to the census returns, there are two dwellings in this area which still exist there today. These are the cottages on the left of the track down near the children's playground in Holyrood Crescent and there is an old barn called Little Sopwell Barn nearby. Sopwell Barnes may also have been part of the farm at New Barnes (Sopwell Home Farm). Some residents remember that there was a piggery down there and that they sold fresh vegetables.

In 1851, George Wetherby an agricultural labourer, was living in one house at Sopwell Barnes with his family; and Thomas Hanshaw was the shepherd living in the other. In 1861, Sopwell Barnes was occupied by Thomas Webb and family – he was the farm bailiff – and Robert Frost, a ploughman and his family. In 1871, John Eames and Thomas Cooper both with their families occupied the dwellings. They described themselves as agricultural labourers.

In 1881, the same farm was called Sopwell Farm and the inhabitants were Thomas Cooper (probably the same one but now describing himself as a shepherd) and his family, and Charles Thrussell, a ploughman and his family. In 1891, William Patten was the shepherd and in the other cottage was Matilda, the widow of Thomas Cooper. She was a laundress.

In 1904, the name Little Sopwell Farm first appears and its boundaries were given as the St Albans Watford railway and Watling Street from where it meets Park Street to the bottom of what is now Doggetts Way by the gasworks.[58] W. Yells was the tenant. In 1911, the tenant was a David Warby, a farm labourer.

Kathy Sinfield:

There was a long avenue of lovely old trees that used to go down to the farm. There are small farm cottages there and they are still there, where the railway line goes over and there's a bridge and it's just down the bottom here – if you follow down from Holyrood past the children's play area there, there are two cottages and they were the cottages for the farm workers. I think that all the ground and fields round there were part of the Gorhambury Estate.

Bill Mackenzie:

That was another little farm down there . . . you go down . . . [to] . . . where the kid's playground is on the right-hand side and follow that path down through the bridge to Butterfield Lane. I used to go to school with a bloke, he lived in Park Street, whether he was just renting it or not I don't know. He had a little business down there, pigs and chickens and stuff like that. He had nothing to do with the farm.

St Julian's Farm

St Julian's Farm was on St Julian's estate owned by the Wilshere family. The main farm buildings, including the tithe barn, were on the west side of Watling Street, where the Tithe Barn estate is now. Most of the fields were in Sopwell. Part of Tavistock Avenue was once called St Julian's Farm estate.

From 1833, the farm was leased to John Gomme. In the tithe map of St Stephen's, part of Wat Mead (watery meadow) and Sopwell Wood field were leased to John Gomme, so these fields must have been part of the farm. Gomme appears in the census records at St Julian's Farm until 1871, when he was seventy-eight years old. The farm was described in the census as having 370 acres, and up to eighteen men and boys were employed there.

In the two following census years of 1881 and 1891, the farmhouse is occupied by William Widdon, who describes himself as a stockman, and his wife. In 1901 and 1911 the farmhouse was once more occupied by the farmer, then James Varcoe. His father, Edwin, also farmed there for some time from 1906 until his death in 1918, aged eighty. In October 1918, in a formal announcement in the newspaper, James Varcoe, a farmer, announced the death of his father Edwin and called for all creditors to give their claims, so it is most likely that the family were still farming there at least until then, and that they owed money!

In the early 1930s, the farm was being run by the Muir family. Betty Terry's mother worked there:

> She used to go cleaning three days a week for Mrs Muir and my husband had a lorry and there was no place to park it, so he got permission to park it in the farm.

Betty Terry described the farm as quite big, with quite a lot of ground:

> We used to go mushrooming in the field behind St Julian's Farm. And a long, long while ago there was an airfield there just beyond the wood in a little private field and I remember it was 10 shillings for a flight. None of us could afford 10 shillings for a flight. I don't know who ran it or anything but they had the flag, you know the yellow flags that they used to put up on each corner of the field, and it was there for quite a while. That was when I was quite young about ten or eleven.

Kathy Sinfield also remembers the Muir family:

> Mr Muir's farm was where Tithe Barn is now. That was a whole farm and he used to have apple trees, orchards. There were just fields right down to where the motorway is now and there were two woods, a little wood and a big one and we used to go blackberrying in Muir's wood and bluebells [were] growing just there and it was lovely. The green going down to the roundabout down Watling Street (Park Street roundabout) that was all clear chalk at the time and the growth that's there now, it's grown.

Margaret Wickens' best friend at secondary school was Mary Muir of St Julian's Farm. Winnie Day worked on St Julian's Farm as a land girl during the Second World War. She looked after the horses and sometimes the cows in the fields where Mandeville School is now. She also delivered the milk for the farm. Bottles have been found at Sopwell Mill Farm with 'Muir St Julian's Farm' inscribed on them.

Bill Mackenzie remembers the farmland:

> I can remember walking up toward Cottonmill over the level crossing right the way up. That was just a path coming straight and we used to turn right on what is Abbots Avenue West now and where Mandeville is and it was all farmland. We used to walk along the boundary of Mandeville along the back of the houses as that was all blackberry bushes. Then we used to come across here down the bottom of the road – that was St Julian's Farm . . . We used to bunk off from St Julian's [School] and walk across the fields, sit in the barn at the farm, then come through the farmyard when the farmer wasn't about . . . It was still a working farm when I left school in 1954. That was when they started building the houses there on the Tithe Barn estate.

There was a massive barn across there. The farm was still working up until 1954 or '55. I am sure it was still there when I left school.

The 'massive barn' was St Julian's Tithe Barn which dated from the fourteenth century. It was dismantled when the estate was built and taken to the Chilterns Open Air Museum awaiting reconstruction.

Margaret Brown got into mischief:

I can remember St Julian's Farm. When I was a kid, I used to go scrumping in the fields. We used to wander when we were kids, we were free to do as you like. There was about four or five of us all used to go off together. We used to go over these fields and across Watling Street. There was a big field there and we used to go and get mushrooms over there and there was the farm at the top with orchards. I was a bit of a tomboy and I was very small compared to the others and I was a bit daring, they always let me do things. Well, they hoisted me up this tree to get these apples. There was me busy shaking this tree and the farmer came down and they all ran off and left me up the tree. In the end the farmer got me down. He got hold of me and shook the life out of me. He said you can just drop that lot you've got, and that was it.

Hedges Farm

Hedges was another farm in the Manor of Sopwell. The farmland in Sopwell adjacent to the North Orbital all belonged to Hedges Farm. Hedges is the only working farm left, part of which is in Sopwell. Many of the fields that used to belong to the other farms have now been taken over by Hedges. When the North Orbital road was built, the farm was cut in half. Nowadays, Hedges, run by the Woollatt family, also rear and butcher their own Hereford beef cattle from home-produced cereal and silage.

In 1766, it was managed by Thomas Ayleward.[59] In the 1851 census, the famer was a Richard Pocock and the farm was described as having 549 acres and employing twenty-two men. In 1864, Francis Robert Silvester, a vetinary surgeon, was given as the farmer of Hedges *and* Sopwell Farms. In the indenture between the Earl of Verulam and Francis Silvester in 1863, the farm was described as consisting of

outhouses, barns, stables, hovels, sheds and other buildings plus several closes, fields, and pieces and parcels of arable land, meadow pasture and wood ground amounting to about 223 acres, 3 roods and fourteen perches.

Silvester was also given the rights of hunting, shooting, sporting and fishing on the land.[60]

In 1893, the Sopwell and Hedges site was considered as the site for the Royal Agricultural Show for the following year. Unfortunately for St Albans it was not chosen.

Bill Mackenzie remembers the cottages:

When I was a kid at school at St Peter's, there was a mate of mine, Robert Wilson. His dad used to keep Hedges Farm up on the North Orbital. Often his mum would come and pick him up and take us up to Hedges Farm. That was nice because you would ride up there in a car but I had to walk all the way home . . . . You would come out of Hedges Farm and, they are probably privately owned now, there are two little flint cottages down in the field and they used to belong to the farm and the head cattleman and another bloke, both farm workers used to live down there. We used to walk all the way down there, over the river, come out in Butterfield Lane and walk right up Cottonmill Lane and Gorham Drive to come home.

The flint cottages are still there on the North Orbital.

Sopwell Nunnery Farm

There are some lovely watercolour images by Buckingham in St Albans Museum which show livestock and farmland adjacent to the Nunnery ruins, so we know there has been a farm there for hundreds of years. All the land surrounding the ruins was used for grazing. It is unlikely that it was cultivated to any extent as the land is predominantly water meadows. The tithe maps reveal that the land was let in parcels to various tenants.

Farm near Sopwell ruins J.H. Buckingham Courtesy St Albans Museum

In the late nineteenth century until at least the 1930s, the parcel of land in front of the ruins in Cottonmill Lane was leased to Charles Pearce. The Pearce family also had a scrap yard there. In one of the buildings they kept cattle and pigs. They also raised chickens. Their longest serving member of staff was Arthur Bailey, who started delivering milk from the farm when he was a boy. The farm's cowman, Alf Willis, was brought over from Amersham to St Albans in around 1869 by Joshua Pearce. Apparently, if you went into the farm area and asked him what the weather was going to be like, he would look up at the sky towards the Abbey and watch the clouds and tell you – and he was invariably correct.[61] Alf, who lived at 24 Longmire Road, was the stockman at the time of the Nunnery Farm fire in 1931 (see Appendix 1).

In 1920, the landowner, the Earl of Verulam, was served with a notice under the Acquisition of Land (Assessment and Compensation) Act 1919 to sell two plots of land amounting to nine and a half acres to be used for building two roads and houses. It was estimated that the value was £400 per acre. The land in question was part of the Nunnery Farm and extended from the area where Nunnery Stables is now as far as the railway (now the Alban Way). Part of the area was called Sportsman's Hall field. Charles Pearce, the tenant of the farm, was using the field as pasture for his animals and he put in a claim for loss of grazing. He had also paid rates on the farm. The claim was settled and he was given £100 compensation. This was probably when the corporation was thinking of extending Prospect Road, although this didn't actually happen until the late 1920s. On the farm were ten horses, fifteen heifers and 37 bullocks.

Stankfield Mill

In medieval times, around the twelfth century, there may have been another mill on the Sopwell stretch of the river called Stankfield, or, Stamford Mill. However, this could have been the former name for the present Sopwell Mill, as it was believed to be further downstream towards the site of New Barnes Mill. The Stankfield and New Barnes mills (mill streams) were said to have provided eels for the Abbey kitchen.[62] Stankfield Mill was rebuilt in 1326–35.

The watercress industry

The river Ver, being a chalk stream and having very pure water, was ideal for growing watercress. Watercress was grown in the Sopwell area until the 1970s. Watercress was known as a 'super food' in the Victorian times and so was in demand. There were watercress beds on either side of the GNR (Hatfield line) bridge, run mainly by two families: Pinnock's and Lee's.

The Pinnock family managed the watercress beds backing on to the gardens in Longmire Road (now Riverside Road) where the Watercress Wildlife Association is today. There is a watercolour by Buckingham of Pinnock's Field, Priory Park so they must have farmed the land before they went into watercress production around the 1880s. Between the wars they dominated the watercress business. It is said that they generated so much rail traffic that the Abbey Flyer line became known locally as the watercress line. Later on, most of the watercress traffic went via the mainline City station. Vera Foster's mother was a member of the Pinnock family. Her granddad rented the beds in Park Street from Lord Verulam and at one time her uncle Doug used to run the watercress beds behind Riverside Road.

The other beds, managed by George Lee, were on the other side of the Hatfield railway line by the Verulam golf course at the New Barnes end.

Vic Foster:

> Lee's was at the back of the Cottonmill Club. If you can imagine going down Cottonmill Lane, you come to the junction at the bottom of Butterfield Lane. As you turn into the original lane on the left-hand side, there is a gate. That was the track that went down behind the Cottonmill Club down to Lee's watercress beds. You can't go down there now because it is private and is fenced off but you went down behind the mill manager's house.

Andy Webb of the Ver Valley Society interviewed a local watercress worker, Gerald Dunham, in 1993. Gerry worked in the watercress industry from 1948 until 1952 and was employed by Mr Pinnock in Riverside Road. At that time his salary was 35 shillings per week. Mr Pinnock, who lived in Albert Street, had worked the watercress beds in Riverside Road all his life. Four of his six sons worked there with him along with four others (including Gerry), so there were nine workers in total. The Riverside Road site also operated as

Right: Watercress bed showing trustle board by Sopwell mill c.1920s Courtesy Margaret Wickens

a market garden supplying vegetables and chickens to the district. There were some small greenhouses for the production of salad crops. The watercress was sold locally and sent by rail to wholesalers in Manchester, Leicester and Rugby.

Gerry said that the best watercress from the Riverside Road beds came from the biggest of the two beds which was known as the 'top-head'. In its later years, the 'top-head' was enlarged considerably and was watered by a number of springs which emerged from the valley's side at its top end – no river water was needed. The water flowed over the 'top-head' through a culvert under the GNR embankment, over two more watercress beds and on into the river downstream from Sopwell Mill Farm. Square wooden pegs were driven into the beds at regular intervals, forming straight lines the length and breadth of the bed. With their flat tops, and protruding three-quarters of an inch above the water, they enabled workers to move over the bed to pick the watercress shoots by means of a series of wooden planks or trustle boards. The men wore waders.

Watercress was harvested once a week, each time from a different part of the beds so that tender new shoots had time to regrow. It was then packed into baskets. The baskets were labelled according to their size, destination and wholesaler. Watercress sent outside the area went via St Albans Midland (City) station. The best price for the watercress was obtained after the Christmas period through January and February and into the spring when the choice of other vegetables was limited. After this, the price and the quality of the cress deteriorated. Less tender

Old watercress beds in Riverside Road 1970s © Peter Wares

shoots were produced as the cress proceeded through its seasonal cycle.

Harvesting ceased between October and December when the beds were cleaned and repaired, and the watercress enters a more dormant stage. Cuttings for the next season's crop were taken from the bushy growth above the water in June or July. Although the Riverside Road beds were of good quality, Gerry said that old Mr Pinnock believed the best watercress in the area came from the beds situated between Kingsbury Mill and Holywell Hill through the area now occupied by the lake in Verulamium.

In 1952, Mr Pinnock retired and the business was taken over by his sons. Gerald and the three other workers were laid off. At the time he was earning £10 and 10 shillings a week. After 1952, the cress beds were worked by a decreasing number of the Pinnock family until about 1972 when Doug Pinnock, the last member of the family to be involved in the industry, sold the site to Mr Lawes. Production ceased between 1970 and '72.

Between 1958 and 1961, Gerry began working the beds on the downstream side of the GNR embankment. He took them over from the other local watercress grower, Mr Lee. Access to this site was also from Riverside Road, via a short tunnel under the railway. For the sum of £40 a year, Gerry rented these beds from the Gorhambury Estate. Apart from cress, Gerry also grew vegetables, mostly potatoes and cabbage, which he sold to Jack Hart's café in Verulam Road (between George Street and Lower Dagnall Street). The watercress was sold locally and also sent by rail to McCarthy's, a wholesaler in Manchester. However, after three years the ground became too wet to grow vegetables – the site was often waterlogged – so Gerry decided to look elsewhere for work. The watercress beds here fell into disuse until around 1980, when Verulam Angling Club acquired them and carried out extensive landscaping alterations to improve the site for fishing. The springs that fed the beds now feed the lakes. In winter when the lakes are frozen, spider's web type cracks appear in places where the spring water melts the ice.

Other residents remember the watercress beds. Steve Peters said that his ancestors were watercress growers living at Sportsman's Hall in the 1840s. He believed the cottages were meant for watercress growers.

Betty Terry:

The lady who lives opposite said her brother-in-law used to work there in the watercress beds. When he left school at fourteen and when the war came he wanted to join up but they wouldn't let him because he was an agricultural worker. And he used to drive the horses and carts to take the watercress and he said a bomb dropped on the watercress beds but I never heard anything of that.

Margaret Wickens:

I would go down and get watercress from the watercress beds, a shilling's-worth, and my mum would sell it off to the neighbours at a profit.

In the 1950s a new sewer was laid past the back doors in Longmire Road. The pipes were very large and the ditch very deep. Pumps worked night and day to pump out the water as the ground was full of springs. A lot of water was diverted from the watercress beds and they dried up and the river dropped. With that the industry ceased. Watercress growing wild may still be seen along some areas of the river.

Old watercress beds between Sopwell Mill and New Barnes Mill 2011 © Sandy Norman

Above and facing:
The Butterfield family of Sopwell Mill Farm in the 1920s
Courtesy Margaret Wickens

Abbey station in front of gasworks 1958
© Brian W. Leslie

Chapter Three
Industry in Sopwell

Until the mid nineteenth century, Sopwell was mainly rural and few people lived there. The Industrial Revolution brought great changes. The arrival of the railways and the gasworks, for example, brought a lot more people into St Albans to live and work, and many of them lived around Sopwell.

The Sopwell Canal?

If all had gone to plan, St Albans could have been linked to the Grand Union Canal and the canal would have gone through Sopwell.

Parts of the river Ver have been canalised, probably since Roman times, which implies that the river used to be much wider and deeper and, therefore, navigable. In the last quarter of the eighteenth century, canals were becoming a popular and cheap means of transporting bulky loads.[63] The Grand Junction Canal Company, considered to be the greatest canal company south of Birmingham, connected the industrial Midlands with London. St Albans, along with many other neighbouring towns, made an application to link with this canal system. The inhabitants of St Albans were obviously anxious not to miss an important trading opportunity. In 1792 and 1793, following public meetings to approve the idea and raise subscriptions, a proposal was put forward, initially by Lord Verulam, to have a navigable cut made to join St Albans to Watford. As can be seen from the plan, it would have passed right through Sopwell. The plan of the cut for the St Albans end was to follow the path of the river coming from Park Street and then to cut the canal from New Barnes Mill through Sopwell Mill and the Cottonmill to Holywell Hill where it would terminate.

Although the idea had popular support, several objections were raised. The Spencer family, descendants of the Duke and Duchess of Marlborough, living in Holywell House, thought the cut was likely to come a little too close to their property for comfort and wanted it reconsidered. Another concern was over a proposed road from the wharf to Sopwell Lane. The St Albans and South Mimms turnpike insisted on having tolls on this road, which was unpopular. More serious opposition came from landowners along the line of the intended cut. They did not want it at all. Neither did the millers who were totally against it. They feared that the canal would draw too much water from their mill streams and so deprive them of power.

Despite all the opposition, a bill was brought to Parliament in February 1794. Four days later a well organised objection was submitted to the House of Commons by the landowners saying that a canal was not necessary as a perfectly good road existed between Watford and St Albans and that the river Lea was navigable to Hertford.[64] Furthermore, they said that the cut would mostly be of local benefit to St Albans at the expense of other neighbouring towns (notably Hertford) and so was not really in the national interest. There appeared to be a certain rivalry between St Albans and Hertford. The bill was lost by just one vote. Undeterred, the canal supporters brought a new bill to the House of Commons on 5th February 1795. More meetings were held in the town hall and more subscriptions were raised. Finally, it went through and received royal assent on 2nd June 1795.[65]

The canal was never cut. There were many political and financial reasons, but probably the overriding cause was the lack of sufficient water. This was a problem the Grand Junction Canal Company faced from the start. They wanted to build a broad canal that could allow barges from the Trent and Thames basins to be able to pass each other, so twice as much water was needed.[66] The highest point of the canal is near Tring where, by a series of locks, it rises to above 30 metres to pass through the Tring Gap at the village of

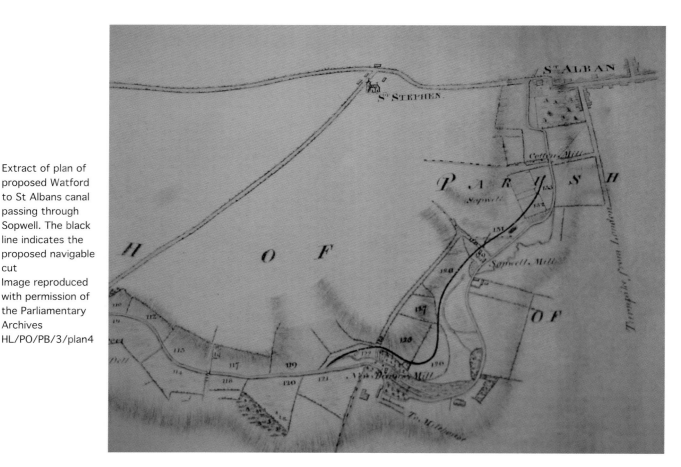

Extract of plan of proposed Watford to St Albans canal passing through Sopwell. The black line indicates the proposed navigable cut
Image reproduced with permission of the Parliamentary Archives
HL/PO/PB/3/plan4

Bulborne. The water shortage here delayed the building of the main trunk of the canal and all the subsequent branches. Some of these branch canals, such as those to Aylesbury and Northampton, were delayed for up to twenty-one years, and there were others, such as the one to St Albans, which were never constructed.[67]

Sopwell would have been completely different had the canal been built, and the town's economic focus would have been on water transport rather than the railways for several decades at least. We may not even have had the Abbey railway line.

The railways

The coming of the railways made a marked change in the economy of St Albans. There was no need for travellers to go by stagecoach which meant that the coaching inns situated on Holywell Hill were no longer vital to travellers. It also meant that routes into the town changed. Travellers arriving from London would no longer have to travel via Old London Road and Sopwell Lane.

The railways provided employment and many more people came to St Albans to work. These people needed housing and so the building of more roads and houses was started. Prospect Road is an example. Many of its original residents worked on the railways. A group of cottages specifically for railway workers was built on Holywell Hill near the Abbey station.

In 1858, a branch line from the London and North Western Railway (LNWR) at Watford was the first railway to come to St Albans. Its terminus was at the bottom of Holywell Hill. Originally the station was called St Albans LNWR and then St Albans LMS – London Midland and Scottish – but was renamed St Albans Abbey station in 1924 so as not to confuse it with St Albans mainline station.

When the railway was first envisaged in St Albans in 1847, the council wanted the LNWR link to go from Watford to St Albans, Luton and Dunstable.[68] That didn't happen, at least not on one line. The engines were originally steam locomotives.

London Road station with engine 1950 © R.F. Roberts

St Albans also had another rail link which terminated in Sopwell. In 1865, a six mile single-track branch line from St Albans to Hatfield, originally run by the Hatfield and St Albans Railway Company, was opened. The line terminated at London Road and the station was called St Albans GNR – Great Northern Railway – and then St Albans LNER – London North Eastern Railway. From Hatfield, one could then take a connection to London. In 1863, in order to build the station, land had to be purchased from Lord Verulam. This land included the London Road Toll Bar which lay on the town side of the station. Keeping it there would have meant that railway passengers and vehicles travelling to and from the station would be subjected to the toll. The railway company negotiated to move it further out and they finally agreed to pay £10 per year to allow free passage for station traffic.[69]

In 1883, the company was absorbed by the Great Northern Railway. In 1923, the line was extended to link up with the London and North West Railway at the Abbey station. These companies were nationalised in 1948 along with all the other rail companies. In July 1950, following nationalisation, St Albans LNER station became St Albans London Road.

When the Hatfield line first started, there were eight trains in each direction and two on Sundays.[70] The line was never really commercially viable. It did not attract many passengers and had to compete with the main line to London when it opened, and later with the buses. It was used more during the Second World War when workers used it to travel to the de Havilland works in Hatfield. Eventually, the line fell victim to Dr Beeching's cuts in the 1960s. The last passenger train ran on 28th September 1951, but it was still used as a goods line until 5th October 1964.

London Road station after lines removed 1975 © Nick Catford

A few years later, the single line track was removed, although nothing was done about the track for some time. British Rail was willing to sell the line for a nominal sum to St Albans District and Welwyn and Hatfield councils, but they were reluctant to purchase it because of the responsibility of maintaining the bridges along its length. Finally, in March 1982, the councils were persuaded to purchase the line in order to convert it into a footpath and cycle route, part of which eventually became known as the Alban Way. At one point a road bypass scheme was being considered on this route. The Alban Way was officially opened in 1988. The London Road station building, still standing in what is now Orient Close, can be seen when walking along the Alban Way.

Several residents can remember the trains running to Hatfield.

Bill Mackenzie:

When I was a kid there used to be about two trains in the morning – not sure whether there used to be a lunchtime one or not – but there were two in the morning and two at night for workers. A lot of the people used to work at de Havilland's in the old days . . . After the trains stopped running, they still used the [London Road] station – I would have been about seventeen or eighteen (1956–7) and I worked for the railway for a little while. Where the [City] station is now, that used to be a railways goods yard and I used to work as a van boy on the lorries and we used to have to go down to the one down London Road. This bloke used to operate out of there. He lived down Prospect Road and he used to have a horse and cart coming out of the London Road station. A firm called Bibby's – a big cattle food company which stored cattle food in the sheds down there – they used to have a lorry locally and [the driver] used to pick [the cattle food] up from down there and then take it to all the farms around the area. That was in use for quite a while after the trains stopped running. My brother-in-law lived down there for a while. There used to be a couple of carriages parked in the sidings for single blokes working on the railway, laying the lines and that. They used to actually live in two or three carriages down there. A firm called Wilkinson's took the yard over and they used to have tanks and armoured cars and all sorts down there – old army surplus – and they used to do them up and sell them.

Locals remember that the tanks and other old army vehicles were sometimes used by film companies. Wilkinson's, which operated in the yard in front of the old station, were still in business during the development of Orient Close. This was in the 1990s.

John Buckingham remembers the return of the de Havilland workers:

Scrap yard in front of London Road station 1982. Note the armoured tanks © John Buckingham

The main thing I can remember about the Hatfield line was the workers' train that used to come home in the evenings and it would stop at the signals at the bottom of the garden. A lot of the local men used to be looking out of the carriages . . . [they] could have quite easily opened the door and . . . dropped out the train and gone over the fence . . . into the bottom of their gardens, but they didn't, they used to sit on the train and go into the Abbey station and walk back. When the passenger trains stopped running, only short coal trains passed by . . . then the majority of the coal came in via the Watford branch.

Gerry Dunham can also remember the row of carriages down by London Road station where the Irishmen stayed when working on the railways. Vic Foster remembers standing under the tiny bridge between Sadleir Road and Monks Close while the large steam engine rumbled over the top. John Buckingham remembers that a train was derailed near the Sadleir Road bridge.

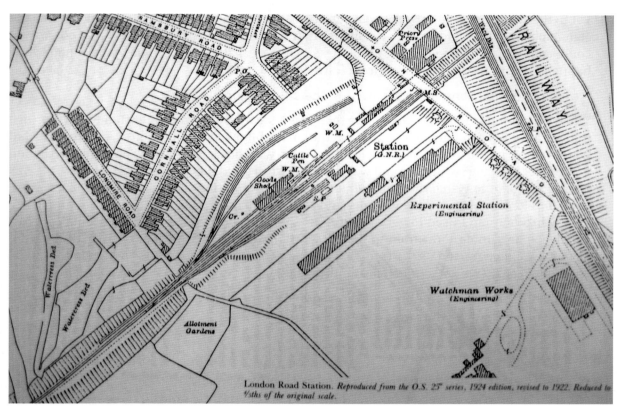

1924 map showing London Road station, Vickers experimental tank and Priory Park

From the mid nineteenth until the mid twentieth century, the Abbey station was a fully functioning station with two rail tracks, a ticket office, five goods sidings, coal yard, cattle pens and goods depot. It even had a women's waiting room. The cost of a ticket to Park Street was 1½d. Joan Forder remembers that it was a proper station with a booking office and a waiting room and seats. People went in to buy tickets in the booking office. The station building was built with white bricks and it had a slate roof, gables and arched windows and a cast iron train shed, originally 160 feet long, spanned the platform.

There used to be a cattle dock which was used in the First World War to house sick and injured military horses on their way to the Royal Army Vetinary Corps equine hospital on St Stephens Hill.[71] This hospital closed at the end of the war and became a veterinary practice which is still in use today. The original gateway is still there. Tom Edgar says that some of the horses were buried in the Hatfield Road cemetery; there is an area in the cemetery which is not used and where it is alleged that horses with anthrax were buried.

John Buckingham says that horses were brought into the station in horse boxes or carriages attached to the end of passenger trains. They came from a big estate in Bricket Wood. He also remembers cattle being brought into the station:

> You had train-loads of cows coming in, animal trains which is hard to believe in my lifetime, all the wagons with little roofs on them and bars down the sides and the cows looking out . . . my mother told me that she remembers that they used to drive them up the road to the market in the town centre when she was young.

Until 1900, there was a turntable at the end of the line and a signal box stood alongside the last house on the left at the far end of St Julians Road. It was dismantled in 1967. This box, which was of standard LNWR design, controlled the junction of the two lines.[72]

Bill Mackenzie remembers how the signals worked:

> You've got the Hatfield line and the Watford branch line, when they both come together . . . there used to be a signal box there. The train would slow – we used to call the Park Street Flyer 'the Coffee Pot', because it had a big tall chimney – and it used to come along there and as it got to the signal box [the driver] had a big ring with a purse on it and he would give that to the signalman and he would go in to the Abbey station to lock the points so that not another train could come in and, going out, they would swap it over again and presumably the same [thing happened] with the bloke coming from Hatfield.

Pamela Marshall remembers watching the steam trains:

> The train running along the Abbey line then was a steam train. We would stand on the bridge as the train went through underneath and the smoke billowed up, then run across the road and watch it emerge the other side, and again go home with blackened faces! Sometimes we stood at the level crossing swing gate and waved at the drivers and they always waved back. This was also a good spot to watch the trains shunting into the shunting shed. The railway banks were good for elephant grass which was nice and slippery, enabling a good slide to the bottom . . .
>
> My brother and I used to get a ride on the signal wire when the train was going past. We could feel the rumble of the train so we knew a train was coming. We used to sit on the line, the signals would go up and as the train went past the smoke came over us and when the signal went down again we got a ride. If my mother knew!

Trains still run from the Abbey station today, although at the time of writing there are plans to replace them with trams.

The gasworks

The gasworks – the St Albans Gas and Water Company – and the railways were closely linked. The gasworks were set up in 1826, which was more than thirty years before the coming of the railway.[73] Before then, coal had to be transported into the city on barges along the canal from Boxmoor and then by horse and cart. When the railways arrived, the industry began to expand and the area around the Abbey station was full of gas machinery and buildings, trucks and coal heaps.

Gas was made by heating the coal until it carbonised, turning it into coke. The coal gas given off was then purified for use. About a hundred wagon loads of coal were used each day for this process. Four gas holders were in use by 1903. According to Kathy Sinfield, two more were built during or after the war.

> It was our playing fields and I was still at school and one August we said what are all these big square holes being dug on the football pitch and they were the foundations (for the gasometers).

Today there are only two gasometers left. These are used as storage for North Sea gas which was introduced in the early seventies. The gasworks closed in 1971 and the buildings were blown up on 5th November 1975.[74] The land was left vacant for many years because of contamination but it was eventually allowed to be developed into the retail site which we have today.

Eywood Road
showing
gasworks
and Mercer
Chronometers
1939
Afl03 61043
English
Heritage
(NMR) RAF
Photography

By the beginning of the twentieth century the gasworks occupied a very large site with some very substantial industrial buildings, railway sidings, cranes and gasometers running alongside the railway and behind a short row of cottages on Holywell Hill.

In the aerial photo above of the gasworks taken in 1939, Eywood Road is shown leading to the bottom end of Wilshere Avenue and Doggetts Way. The building enclosed by the 90 degree angle in the road consisted of two houses, one of which belonged to Mr Osborne who worked as a manager in the gasworks. The first two blocks of houses on the left-hand side of Doggetts Way were gasworks cottages for employees.[75]

In 1951, there were plans to extend the gasworks but the residents of Doggetts Way and Wilshere Avenue drew up a petition and presented it to the St Albans Trades Council protesting against the fumes, dust and smell. They complained about the state of their washing and the effect the dust had on their vegetable gardens. The council referred their complaints to the Eastern Gas Board.[76]

It could not have been very pleasant working at the gasworks. John Buckingham's father started work there before the war:

> He worked on all the retorts in the gasworks in Eywood Road . . . During the war my father used to do double shifts and that was a condition. You would never get people doing that now. The only bonus we got as kids . . . he used to bring us lime juice home, Rose's Lime Juice, and they used to be issued with this once a week. He didn't used to drink a lot of it. He used to drink his tea . . .
>
> Anyway, one Sunday, he took me down there and it was as near to hell as you can get . . . they used to open these oven doors and pull the coke out. You used to stand on a little basin and all the white smouldering was going round and [it] used to go down the conveyor and they used to spray it with water. [The men] were all stripped to the waist. That was hell.

Then he moved on to the second retort which was pre-war, pre-Second World War. He worked in there and then eventually they came into the new one which was opposite Leyland Avenue. That must have been built in the '50s. That was one of the last gas retorts ever built, I believe, in this country. They went initially in white uniforms, boiler suits and within days Dad came home with no hair, no eyebrows, burns . . . and it wasn't as efficient or as good as they said it was.

John, who lived on the gasworks side of Leyland Avenue, had a good view of the activities of the coal lorries:

I used to look out the bedroom window at the gasworks and they were always unloading coal or tipping coke. It's very hard to believe now where all the warehouses and supermarkets are [that] there were great big coal tips and very high. And the lorries used to go up on the top of them and tip the coke out and occasionally a lorry would slide down sometimes tipping over and over before it hit the ground. I don't know how high they were, but they were higher than a house, must have been. There was always something to watch. [It was] a bit dusty. You can still go up in my loft now and find some of the dust, coal dust. They used to occasionally spray the coke down with water but it didn't make a lot of difference. When the scoop used to unload the coal trucks, it used to spin round and open its bucket out and the coal used to go down and the dust used to come over like a cloud. On the last retort, when that was built, it had a revolving line as you might say to lift and turn the trucks upside down to empty them out. It was all done automatically.

View of gasworks and Doggetts Way from top of Holywell Hill G1656_1 Courtesy St Albans Museum

Where Argos and Homebase are now in Griffiths Way, there was a diesel shunting yard where the coal wagons were shunted all around the gasworks site. John Buckingham again:

If you imagine where the fence came down the gasworks right down to the borders of the crossing, there was a diesel shed in there. It used to hold one diesel for shunting around the gasworks. Then they extended it and then they took two diesels in there. The old boy who used to drive them was called Gilly, he came from London Colney. I don't know whether he is with us now, but he knew Dad and he was the one who let us, unofficially and occasionally have rides and do a bit of shunting.

John remembers when the hill above the gasworks was dug out and removed.

Digging out the gasworks that was a big, big excavation. [What was like before it was cut out?] Well, it was just like the side of a hill. If you imagine, from the level crossing without the houses there, you imagine the shape of that hill, you go up the back and see how deep it is where the poplars are. And originally from the crossing, the path that went up there was like an eroded walkway where it used to act as a drain when it rained and there used to be great big oak trees up there . . . to mark the original line of it before Doggetts . . . had the paths put in. [What is Doggetts?] Well Doggetts is that area up there. It was always known as Doggetts, up Doggetts . . . For all this to happen over there, they actually dug out half the hill where Homebase is . . . it was dug into the hill and [the] earth was carted out I believe to Colney Street or somewhere to the pits over there, in the old gravel pits. It used to fascinate me. I used to sit there and lorry after lorry would cart this waste soil out and they levelled it down and they concreted it and put the railway lines in.

Kathy Sinfield remembers the gasworks as being quite frightening. She also remembers them having their own football and cricket teams before the war:

> They had their own sports ground. It had a pavilion and this was at the back of the houses in Doggetts Way – the lower end of the road – and off of St Stephen's. They had their own football team and they had their own cricket team as well. They had a pavilion there and they had a little canteen and it was a wooden trolley bus – the wheels weren't there obviously – and they used to serve tea out of the side of the trolley bus. Mr Ripping who was the St John's ambulance man used to come round at half time with the footballers' lemons. We thought that was great. Half a lemon, they used to give them. And of course the war came along and under the two existing gasometers that was the area where the sports field was.

Lil Day and Betty Cutler also remember what it was like:

> You could hear the retort house. We never had black spot on the roses. Mrs Argent used to say that and she had beautiful roses. When you used to wait for a train to go to Watford it used to smell horrible. We used to go in there with a pram or pushchair to get coke: two shillings for 28lb. We used to do it every week.

Tom Edgar said that you could always smell the gasworks but you got used to it. Brian Currant remembers his class being taken to the gasworks to breathe in the coal tar fumes which were reputedly good for chest conditions. Joan Forder remembers this too:

> We were taken round the gasworks from school, the retort house and all that. We were taken round if they thought you had whooping cough. The coke was sixpence a sack. And the boys used to earn a few coppers because they had their barrows that they would have made and they used to go on Saturday mornings and get a few coppers and then go to Saturday morning pictures.

Tom Edgar:

> The gasworks were always very noisy as well as smelly. There were conveyers going clackety clack carrying fuel and everything else up.

Bill Mackenzie also fetched the coke on a Saturday:

> Where Homebase is now was all part of the gasworks. We used to go down there as kids and it was my job on Saturday morning to take two sacks and go down there on a bike and get coke. As you come up Eywood Road there used to be a sharp right-hand turn, that was the main gate and there was a little office and you went in there and paid your money and they would give you a couple of tickets and then you went out there and a bloke put the thing in a big hopper and when he got 28lb he put it in the sacks . . .

. . . and remembers the retorts:

> You came up Eywood Road from Holywell Hill and you had all the retorts. All the coal used to come in from Hatfield and Watford on the train and it was unloaded and then they burnt the coal and they made coke out of burning the coal. In the winter when it was cold we used to walk along with our hands on the wall. It was lovely and warm as all the retorts were the other side. We used to take our gloves off and put our hands on the wall.

Many children had to get the coke on a Saturday morning. This practice continued until at least the 1950s. Pamela Marshall:

> Every Saturday, it was our job to go to the gasworks and buy a sack of coke and bring it home in the old pushchair. This was a way of earning ninepence to go to Saturday morning pictures at the Odeon in London Road.

The gasworks sold tar oil as a by-product. Tom Edgar said that tar oil if mixed with old engine sump oil was marvellous for coating fences – they would never rot:

> It cost ninepence, and you could go down with a gallon can or a great big drum and they would

fill it up and it was still ninepence. They used to sell that on a Sunday morning. Most people would cart it up the hill on an old pram or trolley of some sort.

Mercer Chronometers

Perhaps the most famous industry in Sopwell was Mercer Chronometers and many Sopwell residents worked there. It started in 1858 when Thomas Mercer established a business in Clerkenwell making marine chronometers. In 1874, he decided to settle his family in St Albans and expand his business. He found a suitable property called Verulam Villa, 18 Prospect Road. This was a five-bedroom town house which he converted into a small factory plus office and living quarters. As business thrived, he built a two-storey workshop of Luton Grey brick at the far end of the garden to cope with increased production and extra staff. It was known by the company as 'the powerhouse'.[77]

By 1907, there was a need to build larger premises because output had increased dramatically. So in 1912, Mercer moved to a purpose-built premises on the corner of Eywood Road and St Stephens Hill, near the gasworks, where they remained until the 1990s. The factory was eventually pulled down and replaced with the Centrium office buildings.

Mercer manufactured marine and survey chronometers which became world renowned for their quality and precision. They made the clocks for famous ocean-going liners including the *Queen Elizabeth*, *Queen Mary*, the *Mauretania* and the Royal Yacht *Britannia*.[78] The main lighthouse at Lisbon harbour has a Mercer clock. The skilled workers employed by Mercer were important for the war effort during both world wars as they were required to increase production to equip the ships.[79] It is said that Mercer was so important in the measuring industry that a particular meter was known as a 'mercer'.

Next to the factory in Eywood Road was a grass field. Tom Edgar said that the grass was kept down by a billy goat. Tom and Valerie gave the goat Spangles sweets. The goat used to wait for them on their way back from RAFA dances in town in the early 1950s; it was addicted to Spangles.

The staff who worked at Mercer all had good things to say about the company. It was a very friendly place to work. Maybe it was a bit relaxed at times as Vic Foster remembers someone who was convicted of counterfeiting £1 coins apparently made at Mercer using their precision equipment. This wasn't long after the £1 coins were introduced (April 1983).

The waterworks

Sopwell had rudimentary waterworks on the river from the late seventeenth century. It is not absolutely clear exactly where they were. Freeman says that they were below Holywell House on Holywell Hill.[80] According to St Albans Museum, the Duchess of Marlborough had them closed down in 1720. This was the time when she was building and landscaping Holywell House. The cotton mill was also known as 'the water house'.[81] A 'Waterworks' is shown clearly on the Dury and Andrews large scale map of St Albans of 1766 as being at Cottonmill.

In 1885, the Holywell water pumping station was opened at the bottom of Holywell Hill by the river. In 1886 an artesian table well of 7½ inches in diameter and 150 feet deep was sunk on site. The tube supplied the new pumping station with 240,000 gallons of water daily from the chalk springs.[82] It became St Albans Waterworks in 1908. According to John Buckingham, they had a big beam engine which pumped the water up via a 15 inch main to the top of the town at Stonecross. The route taken was a gradual one going via Belmont Hill and Keyfield Terrace rather than directly up Holywell Hill.

Pearce's scrap yard

In the 1940s, part of the area near the Nunnery was nicknamed the 'Iron Dump'. It was a scrap yard which nowadays would be called a recycling dump. The Pearce family who owned it are still in business in St Albans with a company called Pearce Recycling. Pearce say they are possibly the oldest family-run business in the area.

The business was founded in 1869 by Joshua Pearce who collected scrap of all sorts. He soon owned a dozen horses and carts and employed ten men to sort the scrap and rags. Joshua owned most of the property between George Street and Lower Dagnall Street. Material was transported to London Road station and then sorted ready for recycling. In 1918, Charles Henry Pearce, one of Joshua's sons, was successful in getting a contract with the War Office to go to France to collect scrap metal. Charles was the first occupant of the Sopwell Nunnery site. He rented the land from the Gorhambury Estate and the Earl of Verulam was listed in the rent book. The rent for six months was £52 10 shillings then. The overspill was sent from Albert Street to the Nunnery site.

Charles died in 1923 and his son Edgar Percy Pearce (Eddie) took over. He lived at Link House Cunningham Avenue. The family farm, Sopwell Nunnery Farm, was in this area too. Pearce used one of his sheds, a large corrugated iron shed measuring 600 feet long, 24 feet high and 14 feet wide, which was near the Nunnery ruins, to store waste paper. Paper was stacked on the bank leading to Prospect Road and was subject to an arson attack in 1931 (see Appendix 1). In the Second World War, Eddie was responsible for collecting scrap metal in Hertfordshire for the war effort.

Pearce had several recycling sites around St Albans. Joanne Pearce recalls:

> Sopwell Nunnery was just one of these sites which used to have metal, although that was much later on, as well as paper brought in there. Albert Street going through to Pageant Road was another. It was the first one with a weighbridge put in and my father, James known as Jim, worked there from 8am to 6pm on the paper side, mostly after the Second World War, and his older brother, Edgar, was running the metals side and doing the accounts, and there is a Pearces Walk in commemoration of this depot![83]

Local residents have many memories of Pearce's, especially when they were children and used it as a playground.

Bill Mackenzie:

> Then you come down to what I call the 'iron dump' which is in the Nunnery. The iron dump was Pearce's. I used to go over there as a kid – great exploring at the weekend when there was nobody working there. It was called Pearce's iron dump but there was all sorts in there . . . I can remember there was just a flint stone building on Pearce's site and they used to store waste paper in it. Where the entrance is to Old Sopwell Gardens, that was on the allotments and there used to be a gateway, a big five-bar gate, going into the field into the allotments.

John Buckingham:

> What used to fascinate us as kids, as we used to walk past it four times a day, [was] seeing all the lorries in and out there . . . In the corner, which was part of our play area – obviously we never went in there when there was any men in there – there was a big old hut in the middle of it where the mound is still, in front of the ruins where they used to sort stuff. In the corner, there were these great big airplane tyres. You could climb up them and go down inside, big bomber tyres . . . it was a bit of a playground . . . There was the old wall which is right round behind the ruins which we used to go along the top of and you could look down into rooms, there were quite a few rooms on that far side. Some of it has collapsed . . . It was also an area full of livestock – a few rats and things . . . [Pearce] took all scrap, paper and rags down there and they had another one up Dagnall Street.
>
> In 1953 when the floods were on, my mother came up with an idea to raise money. She spread it around to collect rags. We used to do this, a little girl and myself. We collected all

these rags and we used to sort them into silks and cottons and wools and go up to Pearce's. We would push an old pram up there with a bag of rags and they would give us some money which went to the flood relief. We got taken up to the town hall, Jean Riley and myself. We had our photographs taken and were on the front of the *Herts Advertiser* . . . and then we were given a box of Smarties® each. We collected, I can't remember how much it was but it was a lot of money in those days – I think it was something like £7. That was a lot of half-crown bags of rags.

Margaret Brown said that Pearce kept pigs and she also remembers an old barn:

Since the war they knocked it down. I think it was when he moved. Because they shifted him out. I think he went along Hatfield Road.

Pauline Crosier:

It was right there in front of the Nunnery ruins. All of that grass was junk yard, full of old cars, wrecks. The ruins were basically ignored. It was all a junk yard right down to where the houses are built now . . . school kids used to cadge ball bearings off them sometimes.

Betty Cutler:

I remember Jos Pearce's, it was a rubbish tip, a tip to look out on – because you couldn't see the Nunnery for rubbish.

Kathy Sinfield and Joan Forder remember Mr Pearce:

The Nunnery grounds were a dump, a rag and bone yard. The railings that had been taken from the houses were still there at the end of the war and never been used. It was old Jos Pearce [more likely to be Eddie]. He used to have a big swelling on his neck. He wore a bowler hat as well didn't he? They have called a place in Albert Street, Pearce's Yard. Where he had his rag and bone, you could take rags down for a penny a bag. He pulled the railings off of every house and when the war ended a lot [of people] went down there and took them back.

Terry Warren remembers working at Pearce's in Cottonmill Lane from 1960 to 1962. His job was to process the scrap iron and send it away to the foundries to build new materials. He said that the site was all gravel and mud roads. The scrap, consisting of iron, steel and swarf (steel which looked like candy floss), was piled so high it completely obscured the ruins. There was a tea hut in the middle. Eventually Pearce moved off the Nunnery site but traces still remain beneath the grass in front of the ruins. When the seats were erected on the Nunnery site, the city archaeologist noted that there was a lot of metal in the soil beneath.

There was another scrap yard by the Abbey station on the corner of Holywell Hill and Eywood Road, until the Abbey View office block was built, and it extended as far as where Sainsbury's is today. J. Charkham, salvage merchants, ran it from 1940 until 1958. Later on it was managed by PCM Metals. Pearce had a small office there for a few years after they left the Nunnery site. This scrap yard closed in the late 1980s and the land was then leased to Sainsbury's.

Today, Pearce own a five-acre site in Acrewood run by Eddie's sons Edgar and James. They went into partnership in 1965 with J.J. Maybank, the largest European waste paper consortium, and they now control 30% of the UK's waste paper industry.

Ryders' Seeds

Just a little way past the Sopwell boundary in Holywell Hill were the offices and exhibition hall of Ryders' Seeds, founded by Samuel Ryder. Ryders' was the first seed mail order company in the country. The seeds were sold at one old penny a packet and were sent all over the world. The building now houses the Café Rouge.

After the war, Kathy Sinfield went to work at Ryders':

Ryders' was a seed firm in St Albans. I went to work there and I think they must have been one of the first mail order companies and that's what I wanted to do. I didn't want to be sewing . . . It was a beautiful building. I used to do despatch to begin with and then when war ended they did a foreign despatch and we sent seeds to South Africa and everywhere and you used to have to have a certificate of germination – you had an inspector down from the Ag. and Fish. to issue a certificate of health. They would take samples. There's a picture in one of the St Albans books of

Mr Clare, he used to get all the seeds ready for the thingamabob and then all the despatch forms for the customs duty and the letter post. I used to do that with a lovely lady called Ruby Churchhouse. There were a lot of old maids there, gentle ladies that had been made widows from the First World War and a lot of unmarried ladies there. On the first of May they would put their straw hats on and on the first of October they would put their silk hats on. They were lovely and I learnt such a lot there. I always thought that I started to learn more after I left school. I certainly enjoyed myself at Ryders'; I learnt such a lot. I worked at Chelsea Flower Show with them and the Ideal Home Exhibition – we used to have a stand there. My first wage in 1945 was £1 and you got nineteen shillings and eightpence because you had your stamp which was fourpence.

The British Cardboard Box Machine Manufacturing Company

Sanitary
Laundry
Belmont Hill
1910
Courtesy
St Albans
Museum

Where the Albeny Gate retirement flats are at the bottom of Thorpe Road on Belmont Hill, there was once a factory making cardboard box packaging. It was owned by the Slade family who also made straw hats and Vic Foster maintains that the boxes were specifically for the hat-making industry. The factory was established there from 1918.

Alfred Bacon got a job there as 'a second boy' in 1921. He said that they used big sheets called strawboard which were scored and shaped and wrapped with paper to make the boxes. Alfred earned thirteen shillings and ninepence for a forty-seven-hour week. Ten years later, he was laid off along with four hundred others during the slump in 1931.[84] In 1987, the land was developed into flats and houses. The houses either side at the Cottonmill Lane end of Riverside Road were built in the 1930s specifically for the workers of this factory.[85] This small housing development, Cottonmill Close, was built before Riverside Road existed.

Before the First World War, the factory site was occupied by a laundry – the Sanitary Laundry (St Albans) Ltd – which opened in 1901. Their premises were described in an advertisement as lofty with spacious workrooms and large open-air drying grounds. They used the best materials with no chemicals and their water came from their own well.[86]

Other industries

At the bottom of St Julians Road, parallel to the railway line, is a yard occupied by a scaffolding firm, Dagmar Scaffolding, which has been there since the mid 1970s. Before that it was occupied by a roofing company.

According to Vic Foster, at the bottom of Holywell Hill there was a radio making company called Photo Precision which made radios for airplanes. This was next door to the waterworks.

Gasworks Field at bottom of Holywell Hill
Undated watercolour by J.H. Buckingham
Courtesy St Albans Museum
No gasworks visible so this may have been Buckingham's vision of what it used to be like

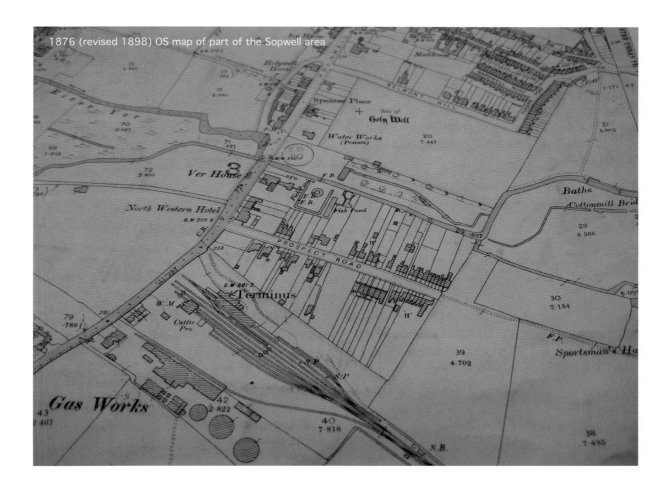

1876 (revised 1898) OS map of part of the Sopwell area

Chapter Four
Footpaths, early roads and pre-war estates

Although most of Sopwell was built up after the Second World War, some roads date from the 1920s and 1930s and others are much older. Those which are most interesting historically and socially are included in this chapter.

Footpaths and stiles

If we look at some of the older maps of the area we can see clearly where the footpaths were. Some of these paths are still in existence. Many of the later estate roads followed the line of the footpaths which linked to important buildings, farms and churches. The 1898 OS map shows that there was a footpath which led from Watling Street, following what is now Vesta Avenue, and down Wilshere Avenue to the gasworks. There still is a footpath which runs in more or less a straight line between Wilshere Avenue and Doggetts Way, between Tavistock Avenue and Maynard Drive down to Mandeville Drive and over Creighton Avenue, down to Holyrood Crescent and over the fields to what was Little Sopwell Farm and beyond. The footpath, depicted on the 1898 OS map from Prospect Road across the Nunnery site and under the old railway line into Cottonmill Lane, is still there although, today, part of it passes through Boleyn Drive and Monks Close.

Trees are shown bordering the paths on the old maps which indicates the old hedgelines. The ancient oak trees on the stretch of the footpath from Creighton Avenue to Holyrood Crescent and down past the children's play area are an example of such a hedgeline.

Kathy Sinfield remembers there were once stiles at the entrances to the footpaths:

> There was an alleyway through to Watling Street – and stiles, loads of stiles . . . at the top of Doggetts, and to get into those fields there was quite a gap. The stile was where the footpath is now. At the top of Maynard Drive where it joins Tavistock Avenue, there was just a little grass opening but there was a field . . . There was a stile going into the fields and there was a stile going into the alley at the back of Tavistock Avenue, two stiles there. [There were stiles the other side] in the field behind the church and one the other end where it went into Watling Street.

Joan Forder says that there were also stiles in the field next to Sopwell Mill Farm:

> We used to come under that little railway bridge that goes to Hatfield and there was a stile, and you could walk across the field, go over another stile and continue down Cottonmill Lane.

Holywell Hill

Holywell Hill, named after the Holy Well, has been in existence probably since Celtic times. The most famous inhabitants were the Duke and Duchess of Marlborough who, at the turn of the eighteenth century, built a house towards the bottom of the hill. After the house was demolished in 1837, the hill became a centre for industry such as the gasworks, railway and waterworks, as well as being a main traffic route.

Another famous inhabitant who lived a bit further down on St Stephens Hill was Isaac Newton Edwards. He was one of the sons of Henry Edwards who bought part of the Holywell estate when Holywell House was demolished. Henry Edwards was well known for electoral bribery, along with his friend, Thomas Blagg, with whom he ran a firm of solicitors in Chequer Street. Blagg was also the Town Clerk. Isaac Newton Edwards trained as a solicitor and later became a partner with Blagg and Edwards. Isaac later became the Borough Treasurer and later the Town Clerk when Blagg died in 1875.

Isaac decided to build a house on St Stephens Hill on land which was once part of the Holywell estate, which he called Westminster Lodge. Part of the entrance lodge, stables and coach house of the original Westminster Lodge still stand and are now occupied by a veterinary practice.[87]

In the late nineteenth century, the Sopwell part of Holywell Hill started to be developed. On the corner of Prospect Road, the North Western Hotel, later to be called the Abbey Tavern, was built. This was a typical Victorian railway hotel. Houses were also built for railway workers. William Buckingham, John's father, was born in one of these three railway cottages. The cottages survived until 1986 when they were demolished to make way for the Abbey View office development. The cottages had not been upgraded since they were built: the only heating was an open fire, the bath was in the kitchen and the toilet was outside.[88]

Another large development was Ver House on the corner of the river side of Prospect Road. This house was occupied by William Hurlock, a successful London tradesman and one time mayor of St Albans. It had

> large and extravagant gardens which contained a fine covered swimming bath with palms and marble statuary, ornate fishponds and a belfry with a fine peal of bells.[89]

These gardens extended along the river behind the back gardens of Prospect Road houses, so they must have been a wonderful sight.

In 1925, after William Hurlock died, Ver House became a hotel for a few years. In 1938, it was demolished and the site was redeveloped to create a roller-skating rink. Pamela Marshall remembers her mother talking about the rink at the bottom of Holywell Hill. Vera Foster's mother remembers it too. The site later housed factories and then a petrol station. Vic Foster remembers the petrol station with a wooden shack in front of it. This was later taken over by the Jet garage. Tom Edgar says that by the river near the garage was a general shop which was often flooded. He also remembers that there was a baker's along that part of the hill. Eventually the garage and the Abbey Tavern were demolished to make way for Latium Close, in 1993, and Aventine Court, in 2002.

North Western Hotel Holywell Hill 1964 Courtesy St Albans Museum

Watling Street

Watling Street is the one of the oldest streets in St Albans. It was once the main highway from London and originally continued on in a straight line over the fields towards the Abbey.[90] The monks of the Abbey had the road diverted in the tenth century, forcing travellers to go down St Stephens Hill, cross over the river and up Holywell Hill into town which was not an easy route to take especially as there was no bridge over the river until the twelfth century. The reason given by the monks was to protect travellers from being attacked by bandits who lived in the ruins of Verulamium. Another more likely reason is that it would have made travellers pass by any markets and tolls in Holywell Hill and so would increase trade to the town – as well as boosting the coffers of the monastery as the monks controlled these markets.[91]

The west side of Watling street was home to St Julian's Hospital, St Julian's mansion which became St Julian's Farm, and the medieval tithe barn of St Julian's. On the other side is St Stephen's Church which is on the north-east corner. Next to the church was the vicarage and then Glebe House. Glebe House still exists but the vicarage had to be demolished because of damage by youths in the 1960s. A bit further down towards where Vesta Avenue is now, there was a house called St Stephen's Cottage which is shown prominently on the 1898 OS map.

In the 1930s, walking towards Vesta Avenue from the church, there were houses called Sherwood, Toorak, Oakwood and Shirley. Then there were numbers 15, 17,19 and 21 and then the numbering jumped to 29 and 31. Then came more named houses: Juliette, Dornford and Highlands.[92] Vicarage Close, off Watling Street was built in the early 1970s on land once occupied by St Stephen's Vicarage.

The first few houses which are set back from Watling Street on what was called St Julians Hill, were built in the late 1930s. They housed American officers in the Second World War.

Old London Road

When the tenth-century monks diverted travellers from Watling Street down St Stephens Hill and up Holywell Hill into town, many chose to enter the town via a less arduous route. A new route was taken from London which came into town via Sopwell Lane. This then became the main highway. It also became part of the original parish boundary. A section of this original highway still remains as a public right of way. It is the footpath which crosses the golf course from Cottonmill Lane and then goes up Riverside Road, past the Jim Green Memorial scout hut and Henrys Grant and along the footpath on the right, then across the Cottonmill Lane/Watson's Walk roundabout through to Sopwell Lane and into Holywell Hill.

This route into town remained until Sir Richard Lee came to live in Sopwell and built his house, Lee Hall, on the Nunnery site. He disliked this route because it bordered his property and he didn't want the general public looking into his garden. So, in 1562, he had the road diverted forcing traffic to pass along what is now Old London Road. This road became the main road into London until the present London Road was built in 1794.

It must have been soon after, at the beginning of the nineteenth century, that the houses in Old London Road were built. These are probably the oldest houses in Sopwell. An estate agent's information sheet for number 71 states that this house was believed to be over two hundred years old. Fern Cottage at number 116 was built in 1858.

Dorothea Bristow lives at Fern Cottage, 116 Old London Road. She runs a B & B and has written a fascinating history of the house for her guests:

> Fern Cottage was built in the year 1858. We know the actual year that [it] was built despite the absence of written records due to an extremely lucky find during the extensive renovation work that was carried out in the mid 1990s. It was discovered that the bricklayer had inscribed the year 1858 into the last brick that he laid right at the top of the chimney stack. Houses were still extremely primitive by modern day standards, with neither running water nor electricity. The original inhabitants of Fern Cottage were lucky though in that they had access to their own well, long since filled in, situated under the driveway of the neighbouring house. Water from this however would still have had to be drawn up and carried inside by means of a bucket.
>
> The earliest written records date from the year 1875 when the property, and a substantial portion of the surrounding land, was owned by George Bidwell and his wife Fanny. These records take the form of an indenture or mortgage taken out by Mr Bidwell along with another gentleman with the familiar name of Mr Isaac Newton Edwards. Not the Isaac Newton we know . . . but a relation of his nonetheless as they were cousins. When George died in April 1881, Fanny inherited his share of the property along with Isaac Newton Edwards retaining the mortgage. However in 1881 he was declared bankrupt. Rumour has it that he had gained huge gambling debts. A Mr Robert Palmer Harding was chief official receiver at the time and in this capacity undertook the sale to a Henry Jenkins Gotto. Gotto was a very colourful character, a Victorian businessman of whom quite a lot is known. Originally, he was a London stationer with his business based in Oxford Street where he amassed enough money to build a huge gothic style three storey mansion at New House Park set in 220 acres of ground.
>
> Gotto was one of the first to advertise his business on London's horse buses and also had a

showcase at The Great Exhibition in 1851 and became the major importer of the new fangled gramophone. He became so well known that he was even featured in a Punch cartoon. On his death in January 1894, his entire estate, including Fern Cottage, was bequeathed to his wife and sons. Sixteen acres of this inheritance were sold later in the year to . . . Jabez Thomas Bennett. In 1897 he in turn sold Fern Cottage and some of the land to an engineer formerly of Kennington Park Road, London who possessed the even more interesting name of Guilo del Rivo. The price had now reached the princely sum of £200 plus interest. Guilo was obviously a bit of an entrepreneur as, in the early 1900's, he arranged for six cottages to be built on the land to the rear of Fern Cottage. These six cottages were then sold altogether for the sum of £1,450.

Through the following years there were a number of different owners, who between them had many diverse occupations, amongst which there was a gardener, a pattern maker and a factory superintendent. It was even owned at one time by Hertfordshire County Council who purchased it by exercising their statutory powers under the Highways Act, at a cost of £14,000, in 1959. The proposal was to demolish the property to allow for the construction of a by-pass, plans, which happily were shelved resulting in the Council selling it on some years later.

During the years many changes to the property and surrounding land have taken place. Sometime after the First World War a grieving widow had the whole exterior of the house completely painted black and the locals nick named it Bleak House. Around the same time, in 1919, a slice of frontage land, 35 foot in length, was sold to the North Metropolitan Electrical Company in order to build a sub-station for the supply of electricity to the area. This enabled Fern Cottage to be illuminated for the first time by the single flick of a switch thus rendering the original gas and oil lamps obsolete.

In the 1920's a large stained glass window was added to the eastern elevation of the house. This now makes an attractive feature in the breakfast room and due to its position allows the room to be flooded with sunshine on bright mornings. However some of the most ambitious changes to the actual structure of the cottage didn't occur until the 1990's when the current owner purchased not only the cottage but also a large plot of ground to the rear of the cottage. This was owned by Mr Mitchell who had bought the plot of land back in 1962 at a cost of £1,000. It was his intention to build twelve lock-up garages, which he then intended to sell or to rent to local residents. The local council however did not approve of his plans and subsequently refused permission for this scheme. Mr Mitchell was unable to think of an alternative use for the land, it effectively being locked in between Fern Cottage and the previously mentioned cottages. On emigrating to Canada a few years later he put all thoughts about it to the back of

Grace (Butterfield) Fitzjohn with daughter Margaret in Old London Road in 1930s
© Margaret Wickens

his mind merely keeping the old deeds and documents as a souvenir. This land then became completely overgrown and almost impenetrable but was discovered one day on a dog walk and on realising that it backed directly onto Fern Cottage the decision was taken to attempt to trace the owner. After many months and much detective work this was amazingly achieved and the strip of land was purchased for £10,000 on the same day as the purchase of Fern Cottage was completed.

The first step of the plan was to use part of the land along with the original side garden to the west to build another house. This was carried out and sold with some of the money then being used to landscape the remainder of the land as a rear garden. The next stage was to submit plans to extend the original cottage. Work for this commenced in October 1998 and was completed in June 1999. The original part of the cottage was then opened as a Bed & Breakfast establishment with the new extended area being used as private quarters for the owner. Fern Cottage is now a locally listed building with a four diamond rating with the English Tourist Board and even has its own website www.ferncottage.uk.net.

Margaret Wickens' family, the Fitzjohns, lived at number 71 Old London Road which is on the north side. Theirs was the only house with a fence. They lived there from 1924 until 1944. The rent for their house in the late 1920s and 1930s was seven shillings a week. A bit further up, at number 87A was Shepherds the baker's. They had a bakery at the back which backed onto Paxton Road and Margaret says that when it rained it often became flooded from both directions. As one of her aunts was married to a baker at Shepherds, she was allowed to watch them making bread. John Buckingham remembers Shepherds:

> In Old London Road we used to look over with envy at the Shepherds bakery – there was a little bakery shop there – and us kids looking in the window . . . and you didn't have any pennies to buy the bits.

Caley's newsagent, tobacconist and sweet shop was also on the north side at numbers 25 and 27. Bill Mackenzie remembers Caley's in the 1940s:

> Opposite the school, there are a couple of steps up Old London Road where the path is high and there used to be a shop there. When I was a kid there used to be two old dears who used to keep it and their brother kept the other shop. That was Caley's. There's no shop there now. It had just a little bow fronted window. The two old dears kept that and then they swapped over. It was a bit of a grocery shop. The other one was an off licence. It got too much for the sisters staying open later so they swapped over. Soon after they went up there, one of them died and then they shut the shop.

Coming from Watsons Walk there were five houses before Caley's and then two or three more before a row of cottages set back with longer front gardens. From number 53 onwards the gardens became much shorter. These cottages (up to number 69) were eventually pulled down when Kingdom Hall was built. The side wall of the end house (69) was in the Fitzjohn's back garden. Margaret's father grew his lilies against it because it was warm.

Old London Road floods 1936 with St Peter's school in background Courtesy Margaret Wickens

In 1936, two freak storms hit St Albans and a lot of damage was caused including flooding in low-lying areas such as Old London Road. Margaret Wickens:

> When I was nearly four years old, there was a terrible storm when the Abbey, amongst other buildings, was struck by lightning and there was extensive flooding. Our cottage in Old London Road sat at the bottom of the road between two hills and we were very badly flooded. What made it worse was at that time there was a fuel station opposite and one of the diesel tanks was lifted by the flood water and overturned spilling diesel into the flood water. Our cottage had coal cellars and my parents were very keen home-made wine makers. They kept their wine on shelves in the cellar and as the water rose the bottles floated off and many of them were broken. Apparently when the firemen went into our cellar to pump it out they were met with a mixture of diesel and alcohol fumes and came up reeling!

On the south (Sopwell) side, there were very few buildings. Coming from Cottonmill Lane, there were Priory Park and St Peter's Schools, the diesel filling station, and next to that the Jim Green Memorial scout hut. Then there was an area of rough land before the Cereals Research Station of the British Flour Millers, St John's Church, a pathway through to Ramsbury Road and then some houses. People say that a smithy stood on the Cottonmill Lane corner, where evangelical meetings took place. However, by the 1950s, according to Kelly's Directory, this was a cabinet maker-cum-carpenter's workshop run by Alfred Joseph Lane whose address was given as 14 Old London Road. Margaret Wickens doubts whether it ever was a smithy as the building is made of wood and so would surely have caught fire. John Buckingham remembers the carpenters:

> Coming home from school – we'd be dismissed and you couldn't get out quick enough – we'd come out the side gate which is now bricked up and you'd come past the old carpenter's shop which stands on the corner of Old London Road and Cottonmill Lane and we were always scared it was going to collapse then and that was all those years ago and it still looks as though it could collapse at any time.

Margaret Wickens can plot all the developments on the south side:

> There were only about four houses on the south side and one of them had a garden which we used as a short cut through to Ramsbury Road. I used to climb up a bank. The first house was next to St John's Church, which no longer exists. There was a little footpath between the cottages and the church, I think it is still there. After the church was pulled down there were more houses built. There was the Cereals Research Station, then there was a field with stinging nettles and that went through to what is now Riverside Road.

The Cereals Research Station closed down in the 1970s and the land was used for housing in the 1980s.

St John's Church was closed in about 1957 despite active support by residents. The church had two stained glass windows, the Good Shepherd and St John the Baptist, which were designed by Francis Skeat in 1934. When the church closed they were removed and taken to St Peter's Church.[93]

Kathy Sinfield remembers St John's Church:

> It was pulled down and there are houses there now. I didn't think they could do that to consecrated ground but it has definitely gone now. The Reverend Bredgley used to come from St Peter's Church to take us for our religious lessons. They had an organ, which the boys used to have to pump, and a corrugated roof.

Mr Fitzjohn, Margaret's father, sang in the St John's Church choir.

Prospect Road

Another one of the oldest inhabited roads in Sopwell is Prospect Road. It was originally a track through the fields until the construction of houses from the Holywell Hill end in the latter half of the nineteenth century, mainly between 1871 and 1878. For about fifty years, the road was a cul-de-sac and ended where St Julians Road is now. The original houses stopped at number 52 on the south side, and 57 on the river side. Through access to Cottonmill Lane continued via a footpath. In 1912, when St Julians Road was being constructed, Prospect Road began to be extended. Some of the land was farmland belonging to the Verulam Estate – part of Sopwell Nunnery Farm. It was requisitioned for building roads and houses as early as 1920, but later correspondence revealed that the land was not used and reverted back to the Verulam Estate.[94] In 1925, the Earl of Verulam was approached to sell it again and Prospect Road finally joined Cottonmill Lane in 1930.[95] The United Women's Homes Association started building in the new Prospect Road and St Julians Road as part of the Homes for Heroes scheme following the end of the First World War.

Margaret Brown's mother had a friend who lived in Prospect Road:

> She said she used to go and visit her friend, not from here because we lived the other side of the town, and she said she used to go over a field there and through a fence to get to the old

part of Prospect Road, so it must have been all fields there then. I remember she said she used to get through a hole in the fence to save her walking all the way round to Holywell Hill. This friend lived in some cottages down there.

Arch erected by William Longmire in garden of 25 Prospect Road 2010 © St Albans District Council

Shortly after the original houses were constructed, William Longmire (after whom Longmire Road was named), a builder and contractor and sometime resident of 25 Prospect Road, was commissioned to extend the chapel at Lincoln's Inn and he moved and re-erected the old arched chapel entrance in the rear of his garden at number 25, where it stands to this day, some 15 feet high.[96]

In the rear garden of number 23 (now 23A), there used to be a thirteenth-century decorated stone window which was removed from the east end of the Presbytery of St Albans Abbey during the refurbishment commissioned by Lord Grimthorpe in the 1890s.[97] Unfortunately, very little of it remains today.

There was a mix of professions living in Prospect Road. In 1881, a retired captain was living at number 1 Aldbury Cottages, and number 2 Aldbury Cottages housed a dairyman. The Shrubbery was occupied by a housekeeper, and in Sunderland Villas there was a nurse and a retired farmer. In Laurel Cottage lived a general labourer and in St Mary's Cottage there was a retired gentleman and his wife. Tower Cottage housed a solicitor's clerk and family, plus boarders, and in Verulam Villa was the famous marine chronometer manufacturer, Thomas Mercer and his family. In the other, unnamed, houses, there was someone living off interest, a retired baker, a railway clerk and a retired draper. It is interesting to note that none of the residents, with the exception of children, were born in St Albans. They all came from outside the area.

Thomas Mercer set up his Marine Chronometer factory in a workshop at the rear of his garden. The workshop remained in commercial use until 2000, when the entire back-land plot was developed for housing. This is now Ashwood Mews and Mercer's original workshop was incorporated into the scheme.[98] A similar development was undertaken in the late 1980s, when the back-land to the rear of numbers 24 to 52 was developed for residential use. This became the Brambles.[99]

More houses had been built by 1891, and many of the residents were now working on the railways and in the gasworks.

At one time, in the 1980s, Prospect Road had a thriving residents association. They met in the Abbey Tavern, which was on the corner of Prospect Road and Holywell Hill where offices are now.

Priory Park[100]

The area covered by Riverside (Longmire) Road, Ramsbury Road, Approach Road and Cornwall Road was called Priory Park because of its proximity to the Sopwell Priory land. Following the Dissolution of the Monasteries, all the land covered by Priory Park was owned by Sir Richard Lee. It was then passed down several generations until 1669 when it was purchased by the Grimston family (see Chapter one: New Barnes House). The Grimstons later became the Earls of Verulam. Much or all of the Priory Park land was originally an orchard. The land passed down to Isabella Worley but, as she had no heirs, her trustees sold the land in 1886 to Henry Jenkins Gotto.[101] He was a well-known local entrepreneur who had other lands and property in St Albans. A family called Bennett bought much of the land from the Gotto family.

A housing estate was planned in 1891, although it was not built until several years later. Before the estate was built there was green space and a clear view of the gasworks. The building land was advertised for sale by auction on 20th February 1896 with an upmarket description:

> ... being situated on high ground with a southern aspect with commanding view over the Ver Valley, the ruins and the cathedral.

The land appears to have been sold in piecemeal plots to various members of the Bennett family and others. It is thought that the fact that the Bennett family came from Cornwall is the reason for Cornwall Road being so called. There are several houses with Cornish names which backs this theory. Approach Road was probably named because it was the entrance to the estate. Why Ramsbury Road is so called is not so obvious, although one of the Bennett family (Jabez Thomas Bennett) lived in a house called 'Ramsbury House' in Granville Road, so this may have been the link.[102] The development of Priory Park was aimed at commuters.[103] The more upmarket roads were Ramsbury, Cornwall and Approach roads. Longmire Road was one of the first to be developed.

Longmire Road

In 1899, records show Longmire Road being connected to public sewers so it can probably be dated from then. It was certainly occupied in 1900 and it appears in *St Albans Street Directory* in 1901. The original numbering of the houses in Longmire Road ran from number 1 on the south-west corner of the cul-de-sac, to number 28, and then from 29 on the north-west corner to number 42. Beyond the cul-de-sac was the medieval London road. The houses were all originally rented out and were workers' cottages. At the bottom of the cul-de-sac was a large house, built in 1901 by the Bennetts, called Trelabe, which was later renamed the Dell.[104] In the census of 1911, Thomas Bennett was calling himself a general dealer. This house had a boat on the river at the bottom of their very large garden. When the house and boat house were demolished, Riverside Close was built on this land in about 1960.

There is some evidence, although not conclusive, that Longmire (Riverside) Road is sited on a Roman road. It was certainly part of the original medieval highway to Barnet and London, part of which now crosses the golf course.

The census records reveal facts about the hard lives of some of the residents. In 1901, George Ford, a bookmaker was living at number 10. He and his wife, Elizabeth, had eight children and three more by 1905. By then, George had removed to Sumpters Farm in Essex, which was an extension of the Poplar, Middlesex workhouse, and three of his children had been admitted to Langley House for pauper children. His wife was admitted to a local asylum near St Albans after a serious domestic violence incident. Hannah Tarbox lived at number 8. She was the head of a family of six and was a charwoman. She also had a lodger. The Salvage family of eight lived at number 29. Alex, the father was a warehouseman. At 31 Longmire Road lived Mary Hooker aged 59, her two daughters and son plus five boarders. One of the boarders was a box-maker and another a straw hat maker.

Number 2 Longmire Road was a general shop from 1901. Later, a laundry was run from numbers 2 and 3. Then it reverted to a shop again which remained trading until 1954. The large house, Trelabe, was also used as business premises at one time. Gerry Dunham remembers the shop:

> There was a dead end there and there was a shop – there was a gap and then there were two houses and the first one was a shop (sweetshop).

The occupations of those living in the street in 1911 give an interesting picture of the industry in the area. They include: plasterers, brush makers, various labourers, gardeners, silk winder, carman, railway plate-layers, coal porter, bricklayer, boot machinist, tin-smith, laundry assistant, and errand boys. There was also a hound-hand and a kennel man. They were most likely employed at the kennels in Cottonmill Lane.

The road gradually acquired a seedy reputation and, by the 1930s, people from the posh end of the estate (Ramsbury Road) were encouraged not to go down Longmire Road. It was a hard rough area of very large families. At one time, there were about two hundred children living in the road. A local man remembers playing 'wars' with the boys from Alma Cut using dustbin lids as shields. There are also suggestions of it being a red light district and that the police and ambulance service vehicles would wait at the corner while the emergency was dealt with.

In the 1950s, the St Albans City band practised in Longmire Road. One of the members of the band, George Wright, recalls that

> The comradeship in the City Band was very good. Practices were on Monday, Wednesday, Friday and Sunday mornings, with some Sunday afternoon practices with the St Albans Light Orchestra. However often some band members would meet up on Tuesdays and Thursdays for a blow. The key to the band room was held at the Wellington public house so it was easily

obtained for some extra practice. Extra practices also took place in the shed at the end of George Peck's garden in Longmire Road, St Albans – band members Ron Slough, George Peck, Nelson Morris and the Bandmaster Herbert Warwick lived in Longmire Road, and soon these extra shed rehearsals became known as the 'Longmire Road Band'![105]

Parts of Longmire Road did not have electricity until the late 1950s or early 1960s (just gas-lights or candles) and there was one elderly resident who still did not have electricity in 1969. By 1968, Longmire Road was quite run down. The houses were among the cheapest properties in St Albans. Proximity to St Albans City station was not an attraction then. However, today, it is a most desirable area in which to live.

In 1970, compulsory purchase of a strip of land allowed a road to be constructed from Longmire Road through Cottonmill Close to join up with Cottonmill Lane. This became Riverside Road. Initially blocks of council flats were built followed gradually by private homes and flats. When the council flats were being built by the river, the close proximity to the water meant that workmen had to use pumps constantly to drain the water which kept filling the foundation trenches.

Cottonmill Lane

Aerial view
of Sopwell
15.3.1949
© English
Heritage.
(NMR)
RAF
Photography

Cottonmill Lane was an important route to the city. However, it wasn't called Cottonmill Lane until the nineteenth century. On a map dated 1634, it was simply called 'the road to Sopwell House'. The road followed a part of Green Lane, an ancient lane which formed part of the town boundary in the middle ages.

The lane extends from Old London Road down as far as the mainline railway bridge roundabout at Mile House Lane and has had some historic buildings along its length: Sportsman's Hall (actually two cottages), the ruins of Lee Hall, Sopwell Mill, New Barnes Mill and Sopwell House Hotel, formerly New Barnes House. The lane closely follows the river and crosses over it twice. Where the open air swimming baths are, now the Sub-Aqua Club, was the cotton mill.

Until the 1930s, as far as we know, only a handful of people lived in Cottonmill Lane. At the beginning of the twentieth century it was still little more than a dirt track.

Cottonmill Lane by
J.H. Buckingham, 1853
Courtesy St Albans
Museum

A fascinating extract from 1900 describes a walk down Cottonmill Lane from the town:

The first turning on the left is then to be taken, and we begin to get clear of the houses. This road leads slightly downhill and crosses the river. Immediately after, the ruins of Sopwell Nunnery will be seen in a field on the left. Dismantled at the time of the Reformation, this Nunnery is now little more than bare walls, though a portion of the old building is still used as an outhouse. The extent of the masonry, which can still be traced shows how important an establishment it was in the days of its prime. From here a path on the right will be seen to cross the meadows. It starts at a point just beyond some cottages on the right, and exactly opposite the ruins. This leads across two meadows (giving an excellent view of the Cathedral and town), and then enters a short street which must be followed till it reaches a main road. This is Holywell Hill.[106]

It is interesting to note that the ruins are erroneously called the Sopwell Nunnery ruins. The outhouse was probably part of Pearce's scrap yard and farm. The path on the right opposite the ruins was a footpath across the allotments joining Prospect Road.

Betty Cutler, who lived in Cottonmill Crescent, remembers what the lane was like in 1930s:

When I was seven, I had a fairy cycle and I used to come over the river by the baths, There were allotments either side – a very narrow little lane, just over one car width. The river was still there and the bridge but it was a different bridge then, it was a smaller bridge. It was a bit more than a hump.

John Buckingham remembers horses in the field south of the bridge over the Ver. This would be near where the new steps down to the Ver Valley walkway are now. He thinks the horses belonged to Shepherds the bakers.

The lane was very narrow at one time and there were no footpaths either side. In those days road traffic was very light. Bill Mackenzie recalls:

When I lived in Cottonmill Crescent [in the 1940s], there were only two cars, one bloke was a commercial traveller and another bloke actually owned his car – he was posh!

Margaret Brown remembers what they grew in the fields around:

The top field was potatoes – where Trumpington Drive is. The buttercup field went over by the railway. Where the lane comes round, Priory Walk, after that they used to have wheat because my mum used to go gleaning over there for the chickens. Over the railway they used to grow some wheat and stuff and then potatoes. On the hill that goes down into Park Street, well, the potatoes used to go right to the top hill and after that it used to be wheat to the North Orbital.

Cottonmill,
Footbridge
over the Ver
Undated
watercolour by
J.H. Buckingham
Courtesy
St Albans
Museum
Two
footbridges
depicted plus
the mill and
the river

Sportsman's Hall and the stables

In the 1897 OS map of St Albans, Sportsman's Hall appears roughly where the Cottonmill Lane allotments are now. There were two cottages there, probably used for agricultural labourers, and these were always referred to as Sportsman's Hall cottages. The puzzle is, why were two humble little cottages given such a grand name? Nobody seems to know whether there was an actual hall or whether it just referred to the cottages in an area called Sportsman's Hall. The cottages were demolished in the 1950s and replaced by the present apartment block, still called Sportsman's Hall.

The earliest reference found concerning Sportsman's Hall was in 1818, when the household furniture from Sportsman's Hall belonging to a Mrs Collins was sold by auction. This included a hayrick and in-calf cows. Mrs Collins was described as 'leaving business' at Sportsman's Hall near the Cottonmill, St Albans.[107] What the business was is not known, but presumably it had something to do with farming.

There is obviously a sporting connection. The area known as Sportsman's Hall is opposite where the Nunnery would have been and we know that Juliana Berners who lived at the Nunnery was thought to have written a book on field sports. Perhaps the area was used for hunting and hawking? It was certainly used for angling as the river was a lot wider and deeper in the fifteenth century when she wrote her *Boke of St Albans*. Another clue is the Hare and Hounds pub just up the road in Sopwell Lane. The Hare and Hounds dates from 1672.

Sportsman's Hall is likely, therefore, to refer to the hunt or the chase. Fox hunting in the eighteenth and nineteenth centuries was very fashionable and popular, and hunting definitely took place in St Albans, and in that area. The hunt may have been part of the Old Berkeley Hunt. There is a reference to the term 'Sportsman's Hall' in the following extract from *Fox Hunting in the past* which backs up this theory:

> The jovial fox-hunters portrayed by Rowlandson belong to the rough and tumble days of the chase, when hardships in the pursuit by day, and hard drinking when the 'brush' was brought to 'Sportsman's Hall', were the order of the programme . . .

To add to this theory, there were definitely stables and kennels on the site on or near where Nunnery Stables is now. They housed horses and hounds for the hunt in the early twentieth century. John Buckingham's father worked in the kennels in the 1920s and rode with the hunt:

> . . . when he left school he went down to work at the kennels with a man I believe was his employer, called Fenny or Fennies, I am sure he used to say Fenny. He worked there for a few years. I have pictures of him with his favourite little fox cub and favourite little terrier. He wasn't a cruel man, my father. He would never see anything suffer. He used to go with the hunts because he used to ride horses and he used to have a favourite horse. When it got to a river, it would sit down. I always remember him telling me that. [Was there a huntsman there?] I don't recall that because there was the kennels and the building above, Sportsman's Hall. Whether the huntsman lived in there I don't know. I don't remember him ever saying about huntsmen . . . They used to go out in their red togs. Somebody said that the hunt used to go over to Wall Hall . . . and if you think of it you can go right through the valley to it. It's not so far and that's the sort of day they would have [had] – the hounds and the hunt pack cutting through. They would have gone over Brown's Farm, following the river basically and they could have cut through . . .

From 1924 to 1928, P.J. Fenn was a riding master in the stables in Cottonmill Lane in Sportsman's Hall so he is likely to have been the Fenny referred to above. In 1931–2 a Mrs Duncan ran a riding school in Cottonmill Lane in the stables opposite the ruins.[108]

In the census for 1851, one of the Sportsman's Hall cottages housed an agricultural labourer, his wife and children, and in the other was a journeyman miller and his family. They probably worked at Sopwell Mill and farm as that is close by. In 1901, the first cottage

The stables in Cottonmill Lane with the hounds and 'Fenny' 1920s Courtesy John Buckingham

was occupied by John Saunders and family, a railway worker, and in the other cottage was Benjamin Atkins, a gas-fitter, and his family. Later, in 1906, one of the cottages in Sportsman's Hall was occupied by a Thomas and Benjamin Atkins and family, a gardener and nurseryman, and the other by George Butterfield, a farmer.[109] George Butterfield was the farmer and miller at Sopwell Mill Farm. According to his family, he may not have actually lived there but used it for his farm labourers. In 1911, Thomas Atkins was still there.

Many residents remember the original cottages, the kennels and the stables. The cottages were very old and tiny and the toilets were in the garden. The gardens ran down to the stables.

Betty Cutler:

. . . there used to be two little cottages because I can remember them – they got pulled down afterwards because my father went in when they were made into two flats on the corner of Prospect Road. Dad went in the top flat in the newly built Sportsman's Hall. I used to like going up there because you had the view of Prospect Road, coming up the lane, going down the lane – it was a really, really nice flat. They lived there a good many years . . . Opposite [Jos Pearce's] years ago, there used to be a riding stables there with beautiful horses and hounds. Every day, they used to walk those hounds. Duncan I think their name was – they lived in London Road. They were posh people . . . it used to worry me to death coming up Cottonmill Lane in case he'd got the hounds out. He used to walk them because there were all fields round here, and then on hunt days, they used to collect there.

Kathy Sinfield:

. . . the stables were where Nunnery Stables are now and they had packs of hounds and the hunt used to go from there so they must have had some horses there too. I can remember them going out in their red coats and I think his name was Fenny and the flats at the top where Sportsman's Hall is I think they belonged to them. They knocked them down and built the flats. It was Sportsman's Hall originally. That's on the corner of Prospect Road.

Margaret Brown:

There was one old lady who lived in one [of the cottages] for years but next to it there was a family living there right up to when they knocked them down. They might have been two up two down but if they were they were very small, with little tiny windows. They were in a bit of a state when they pulled them down. There could only have been one room with a tiny kitchen on the back.

At the bottom of the hill there was a big stables where they kept the hounds. I can't remember his name but I can picture him: he was a little old man, a bandy little man. He looked like a man that stables horses. [Although] they used to stable a few horses there, it was mainly the hounds he had there. But I don't know who he was keeping the hounds for, could it have been Lord Verulam? . . . My sports teacher from Beaumont School used to keep her horse down there and her name was Miss Woods . . . I never saw the hunt. We used to see them go off with the hounds but where they went to I don't know. He used to drive them, he never took them in vans. He used to take them along the road. He must have gone down Prospect Road.

Bill Mackenzie:

On the right where the little stable mews is [Nunnery Stables], I don't know where the name came from but we used to call it Fenny's stables [as] he was the chap that owned it. The wood at the back of the Nunnery, we always called that Fenny's Wood. Where the name Fenny came from I don't know. I always knew it as Fenny's Wood and Fenny's Stables.

Gerry Dunham also remembers Mr Fenny dressed in his hunting gear. John Buckingham says that the stables were being used until the 1950s but the kennels and the hounds were long gone. The land was then used as a car park until Nunnery Stables was built.

William Buckingham at the kennels with pet hound and fox 1920 Courtesy John Buckingham

Cottonmill Crescent and Cottonmill Close

The first road to be built off Cottonmill Lane was Cottonmill Crescent which was built in 1928 on land formerly used for allotments. Betty Cutler lived at number 29. This was a council house with three bedrooms, a large living room, scullery, bathroom and inside toilet. They had gas lighting. Cooking took place on a kitchen range and that was the only heating in the house. The rent in 1934 was twelve shillings a week. Her father was only earning £3 per week. She can remember all those who lived in the crescent:

Dot and Ron Giddings lived next door, the Laws, Salvide, Braziers and Miss Gurney and Brian at 27. Mr and Mrs Giddings did the washing for mum when she was ill. This was all by hand as there were no machines then.

There was also a road almost opposite called Cottonmill Close. This later became the beginning of Riverside Road. The houses in Cottonmill Close were built for the workers in the British Cardboard Box machine factory in Belmont Hill. On a 1634 map, the area bordered by Old London Road, Cottonmill Lane, the river and Thorpe Road (where Cottonmill Crescent now sits) was called Bing's Orchard. The old borough boundary line went right through Bing's Orchard, through where Cottonmill Close used to be, and joined up with the old medieval highway to London.

Before Riverside Road was built, anyone wanting to get to Longmire Road had to go down Old London Road and down Cornwall Road. There was a footpath but no traffic could get through. Further down from Cottonmill Close were fields and allotments.

Mentmore estate and beyond

In 1935, Leyland Avenue was built and in 1938–9, just before the war, the Mentmore estate (Mentmore Road, Boleyn Drive, Sadleir Road and Nunnery Close) was built. Joan Forder, who lived in Boleyn Drive, remembers that the war had started before they finished building the road and it was still just cobbles until the '50s when she got married. Margaret Brown also remembers:

> The war came and they hadn't quite finished the estate so they had to rush and finish it. They couldn't sell the houses so they let a lot of them to start with because people wouldn't buy being late like that. This road [Boleyn Drive] was never made up. It was still rough, great big flint stones, until about 1950. The houses were built by Janes the builders from Luton and the lady (who lived at number 3), she kept a brochure of the house. It was £30 down and so much a month for the mortgage. The £30 covered all the solicitor's fees and road charges. After war when the road needed making up, the council wanted everybody to pay but because she had kept the brochure, Janes had to pay for it. There were piles of paving stones at the bottom of the road ready to do this road but they never did it because the war came. Those piles of paving stones stayed all through the war and after the war, they were still down there and nobody touched them.

After the Mentmore estate was built, it was all fields until Park Street. Margaret Brown again:

> It was all fields over the back there. The lane went down as far as the level crossing . . . round the lane over the back here, we used to call it the buttercup field because it was one big mass of buttercups – where Monks Close is now – and that's all there was round there. It was a real narrow lane.

Several people remember two cottages which appear to have been situated near where Old Oak is now. Vera Foster who lived in the flats opposite Abbots Avenue between 1949 and 1953 remembers them. They had very narrow windows and pebble-dash rendered walls.

> Down the road there were these two farm cottages and somebody got evicted from there and it is the first time I have ever seen anyone with all their possession out on the street. Neighbours took them in overnight. There was no Cottonmill Club there then. There was nothing there. There was no entrance through to the field.

Margaret Brown:

> There were two houses further along [Cottonmill Lane] that belonged to the farm. They weren't old worldly. They looked as though they were built in the 1920s or early '30s as they weren't old. They were there when we moved in here. They were quite decent houses.

There was another, larger, red-brick detached house a bit further down. Vic and Vera Foster say that it was the mill manager's house. It had a gate and at one time the owner kept great danes, which scared the children passing by so much so that they took detours around Gorham Drive to avoid them!

Joan Forder:

There was a big old house down Cottonmill Lane. Posh people lived there, I don't know who they were. You go down Cottonmill Lane, you go over the railway bridge and before you get to the river on the left-hand side there was a big house. You scrambled up the bank and looked over the wicker fence and there was this big house.

Betty Cutler remembers that it had a pear tree in the garden.

The last houses in Cottonmill Lane, on the corner of what is now Butterfield Lane before it goes over the river, were cottages for the workers in Sopwell House. Betty Terry remembers that in the 1930s one was occupied by the gardener and the other a chauffeur. Today the cottages have been combined into one residence.

St Julian's estate

Until 1931, it was all fields above the gasworks. A footpath leading from Eywood Road up the hill over the fields became Wilshere Avenue and Doggetts Way. These two roads were called the Eywood estate, which became part of the St Julian's estate. The Workmen's Housing Association erected 134 houses with a government subsidy on the site, some of them belonging to St Albans City Council.[110] Kathy Sinfield lived in Doggetts Way:

... the agents collecting the rents were Rumball and Edwards who used to have an office in St Peter's Street up by the church ... The rent man used to come on Monday mornings, Mr Wright his name was, and the houses were 10 shillings a week for a non-parlour and twelve shillings and sixpence if you had a parlour. That was a lot of money then. I had three brothers and three sisters and with Mum and Dad we were the poorest lot in the street and things were pretty rough then. There were no little treats, you had a pair of sandals that lasted you all the summer and it was lovely in September when you got a pair of shoes to go to school in.

Doggetts field with gasworks, Abbey station, Prospect Road and St Julian's Road in foreground c. 1920s © English Heritage. NMR Aerofilms Collection

The houses all had three bedrooms, a bathroom, and fair-sized gardens, and were built of dull red brick with tiles to tone, and partly stuccoed. The rents when they were first built were eight shillings and sixpence per week for the parlour type and six shillings and sixpence per week for the non-parlour type. The houses were not all rented, some were built for sale.

Wilshere Avenue was named after the Wilshere family who were the owners of the Eywood estate and had been since the early nineteenth century. At the time the road was built, the owner was Alice Augusta Wilshere. John Doggett was a mayor of St Albans in 1675 so Doggetts Way is probably named after him. There was also a field called Doggetts Field or just 'Doggetts' which, according to Kathy Sinfield, was at the top of the hill overlooking the gasworks. The grassy area by the path between Trumpington Drive and Maynard Drive, where the line of poplar trees is now, was probably part of it. Margaret Wickens said that one of her favourite areas for picking elderberries with her mother was Doggetts. She describes it as being the fields on the hill over the other side of the railway crossing (Sainsbury's side). She said that if they carried on long enough they would go downhill again towards the river, so it looks like Doggetts was the hill itself. Doggetts Way is the way up to the hill.

Tom Edgar recalls that the council awarded prizes for the best kept garden and that almost all the houses in Doggetts Way had well kept gardens. The house at the bottom of Doggetts Way had a much bigger garden.

> It was always a showpiece. You could see a lot more of what he did there. He had a vegetable patch which was symmetrical and beautifully done. In those days you would never have been allowed to put a car on a drive. Well, there were no drives.

Kathy Sinfield remembers living in 17 Doggetts Way, which is on the left-hand side going up:

> That was Mrs Lewis, that was a Miss Hewitson, that was Mrs Rolls, that was Mrs Lake, that was Mrs Alwood, that was Mrs Harding . . . The houses at the beginning [of the road] are gasworks buildings and [there was an] alleyway that went at the back of the gardens and they had a football pitch.

Wilshere Avenue originally extended from the bottom of the hill as far as Watling Street. After the war it was separated and the top half became Vesta Avenue.
Kathy Sinfield:

> Wilshere Avenue and Vesta were there, except it wasn't Vesta, as Wilshere Avenue went from the bottom of the hill right to Watling Street, and I've got a friend who was born I think in 113 Wilshere Avenue . . . Wilshere Avenue ends at 61 or 60 something so on her birth certificate it's got Wilshere Avenue but she was living in Vesta. After the war the council took over the housing and they separated it in about 1946 and the council took over Wilshere, Doggetts and Vesta. I didn't realise it was all Wilshere Avenue at the time until Pat Harmer used to live – until the last three years – in the same house.

Doggetts Way and Wilshere Avenue stood on their own for three years before Tavistock Avenue was built. Tavistock Avenue was once part of Doggetts Road. Then it was called St Julian's Farm Estate on East Road, while the houses were being constructed, as the land was also part of the St Julian's estate. The land was sold in 1932 to Vesta Finance and encompassed all the land above the footpath between the top of Doggetts Way and Wilshere Avenue before it joins Watling Street. Not all of Tavistock Avenue was included in this parcel. It appears to end at the footpath further up (by number 59).

The houses in Tavistock Avenue were built in 1934. The end nearest Doggetts Way had garages integral to the houses but not so the other end. Mrs Olive Cooper, who lived in number 21 from when they were first built, maintained that this was because the builders ran out of money.

Tom Edgar's future wife, Valerie Millman, lived at number 7 Tavistock Avenue, which is on the left-hand side coming up from Doggetts Way. The Millmans lived there from 1937 until the 1980s. Most of the houses were rented and they paid £1 per week. Tom remembers that beyond the gardens at the back of Tavistock Avenue it was mostly hawthorn scrubland in fields where there were cows. On that side of the avenue, there was, and still is, a footpath at the back.

> The footpath is only there because Valerie's mother rang the council up when they were building Maynard Drive. They took the fencing for the houses in Maynard Drive to back on to the fencing in Tavistock Avenue. She rang them and said do you know there is a footpath there and they said no. Then they checked their plans and came back and were quickly pulling the fencing down.

Tom remembers that there was no central heating in the Tavistock Avenue house so they had paraffin stoves. They bought Esso Blue or Aladdin Pink paraffin from the ironmongers in Vesta Avenue. The lighting was very primitive:

> They had these tiny two pin plugs and to do the ironing they used to plug a socket into the lamp from the ceiling.

In the fifties, Tom Edgar witnessed the building of another house in Tavistock Avenue (2A) in an open space next to the alleyway between Doggetts Way and Wilshere Avenue

> ... which everybody knew as the crystal palace because it had so many windows.

He and his fiancée did their courting in the alleyway where Praetorian Court is now because he says it was nice and quiet. That was in 1953–4.

Vesta Avenue is most probably named after Vesta Finance. They had offices in Tavistock Street, which might be why Tavistock Avenue is so named.

Tony Spear and his wife, Betty, lived at 19 Tavistock Avenue from 1964. Tony was a radio enthusiast and had a very tall mast in his garden. Betty said she was a 'wireless widow'. He was one of the first people to track Russia's first artificial satellite, Sputnik, in 1957.

Grace Muriel Abbeyfield House in Tavistock Avenue is a purpose-built residential home for the elderly. The Abbeyfield Society was founded in Bermondsey in 1956 to help alleviate the problems of the appalling housing conditions of the elderly. In 1960, a branch of the society was formed in St Albans where their first residential house was opened in Stanhope Road. Discussions took place in 1966–7 about building a purpose built residential home. Much of the finance for this venture came from the estate of Grace Muriel Payne, the wife of a local antique dealer who was anxious to help the society. The site in Tavistock Avenue, which had recently been cleared of prefabs, was seen as the most suitable position and, in 1971, building commenced. The house was opened in 1972.[111] It was later extended to provide for an Extra Care section. Some of the money raised came from local groups who took part in sponsored walks.

Mereden Court, the council-run sheltered housing apartments, was intended originally to be a private block of flats but the builders ran out of money and so the council took over the project.

Where the last shop ended in Vesta Avenue, the road became a footpath across an open space. Now this is Watling View, but it was once called Norman Close, probably when the prefabs were built.

Together with a

Freehold Shop and Messuage

No. 1 Shop (Plot No. 1) Wilshere Avenue

Containing :—

ON THE FIRST FLOOR.—Three good Bedrooms ; Boxroom ; Bathroom, fitted bath and lavatory basin, W.C.

ON THE GROUND FLOOR.—Double-fronted Shop, 36 ft. 2 in. by 27 ft. 6 in. ; Parlour ; Kitchenette ; Coal cellar ; Outside W.C.

SCHEDULE OF WEEKLY RENTS

1 to 15 (odd) 33 and 35; 2, 6 and 14 (with garages) and 16 to 46 (even)	Tavistock Avenue, 29 at £1 each or...	£29 0 0
21	Tavistock Avenue	£1 0 6
25 and 29	Tavistock Avenue (with garages), £1 3 6 and £1 4 0	£2 7 6
4, 8, 10 and 12 ...	Tavistock Avenue, 4 at 17/6 let without garages, 4 garages at 2/6	£3 10 0 £0 10 0
104, 105, 124, 125 ...	Wilshere Avenue (with garages), 4 at £1 2 9	£4 11 0

Tavistock Avenue and Wilshere Avenue sale particulars 1935
Courtesy Herts Archive and Library Service

Containing :—

ON THE FIRST FLOOR.—Three good Bedrooms ; Boxroom ; Bathroom, fitted bath and lavatory basin, W.C.

ON THE GROUND FLOOR.—Double-fronted Shop, 36 ft. 2 in. by 27 ft. 6 in. ; Parlour ; Kitchenette ; Coal cellar ; Outside W.C.

SCHEDULE OF WEEKLY RENTS

1 to 15 (odd) 33 and 35; 2, 6 and 14 (with garages) and 16 to 46 (even)	Tavistock Avenue, 29 at £1 each or...	£29 0 0
21	Tavistock Avenue	£1 0 6
25 and 29	Tavistock Avenue (with garages), £1 3 6 and £1 4 0	£2 7 6
4, 8, 10 and 12 ...	Tavistock Avenue, 4 at 17/6 let without garages, 4 garages at 2/6	£3 10 0 £0 10 0
104, 105, 124, 125 ...	Wilshere Avenue (with garages), 4 at £1 2 9	£4 11 0
116 and 117	Wilshere Avenue (with garages), 2 at £1 1 0	£2 2 0
106, 114, 122 and 123	Wilshere Avenue, 4 at 19/9	£3 19 0
100, 101, 102, 108, 110, 111, 115, 120 ...	Wilshere Avenue, 8 at 19/6... ...	£7 16 0
121	Wilshere Avenue, 1 at 18/6 ...	£0 18 6
103, 109, 119	Wilshere Avenue, 3 at 18/- ...	£2 14 0
126 to 132	Wilshere Avenue, 7 at 17/6 let without garages ... ... 7 garages at 2/6	£6 2 6 £0 17 6
211 to 214	Wilshere Avenue, 4 at £1	£4 0 0
96 and 97	Wilshere Avenue, 2 at £1 4 0 ...	£2 8 0
No. 1 (Shop)	Wilshere Avenue	£1 12 0

Total actual and estimated rents per week   £73 8 6

OR PER ANNUM ... £3,818 2 0

Tenants paying rates.

Tavistock Avenue and Wilshere Avenue sale particulars 1935
Courtesy Herts Archive and Library Service

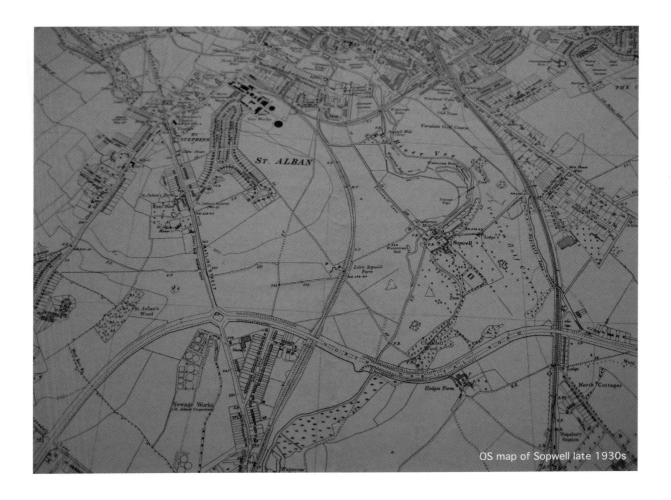

OS map of Sopwell late 1930s

Chapter Five
Sopwell at war

The Second World War is still a very vivid memory for many Sopwell residents. Fortunately, and surprisingly, there was hardly any war damage in the area although we were on the flight path of the German bombers. Betty Cutler remembers the night Coventry was bombed as the planes seemed to be using the Abbey as a marker and then going straight up north. She said that they droned overhead all night long.

Many of the women interviewed, who were children or young adults at the time, felt they had a good war as it did not affect them that much and opportunities arose for them to be useful and help the war effort.

Margaret Brown:

> We used to wander miles. We used to take a bottle of lemonade and a few sandwiches and we'd be off. We never gave a thought about the war. We didn't worry too much.

Winnie Day was a land girl during the war. She worked on St Julian's Farm looking after the cows and delivering the milk. Sometimes she was asked to milk the cows which were kept in the field opposite Mandeville Drive where the school is now. Winnie was also responsible for looking after the farm horses and she often took them to the farriers near St Peter's Church to be shod.

Kathy Sinfield worked in Forsyth's in Chequer Street:

> When I left school the war was still on and you had to do war work. They had some vacancies in Chequer Street, Forsyth's, and they were hat makers and of course during the war they had

to go from fashion into military and they used to do the naval hats and there was a lot of sewing to do there and that went on quite a long time. Obviously now it's the Maltings.

Betty Cutler's father was a member of the Home Guard. Her brother worked at the British Cardboard Box machine factory in Thorpe Road and their friend, Jack, went to work at Eversheds printing waxed milk bottle tops. Betty met her husband when she started work.

He worked at a little shadow factory of de Havilland's next to the golf course. He didn't get called up because he'd got bad eyesight. A lot of the departments were sent to little factories like that. Ours was on the golf links near the iron bridge where there used to be a little factory and I made ammunition boxes for Mosquitoes. All the members were cut to size, put in a jig and glued and screwed together. I enjoyed it there. I earned more money too as we worked on piece work. My husband came from Hendon and he got sent there.

Bill Mackenzie's mother also worked in a factory, the Electrical Apparatus Company (EAC), on the North Orbital estate:

I can remember the North Orbital estate as one big factory. You go up the lane past Sopwell Manor and you turn right before you get to the railway bridge, Napsbury Lane, you go over the railway bridge and in those days as soon as you went over the railway bridge you turned left and that was a gate into EAC – that was the works' entrance. The office entrance was New Barnes Avenue which is the other side of the railway bridge. There was a block end road and there was a gate there and that was where the office entrance was. The whole thing was just one big factory. They used to make switchboards, my mum worked there during the war. They made switchgear and that for all sorts of tanks and aircraft and all sorts of electrical stuff. And another little place up New Camp Road the back of the Maltings. If you come up Marlborough Road and turn left into the Maltings car park where those new houses are there used to be a little left-hand turn, Westbourne Terrace I think it was called and there was a firm there called Switchboards, well that was all part of EAC. There was a factory there.

Many residents remember there was a gun emplacement with a searchlight near where the junction of Nuns Lane and Cottonmill Lane is now, which was run by the ATS. Kathy Sinfield:

Down Butterfield Lane now, of course that was all fields and that and there was a searchlight battery in it and the ATS girls manned the searchlights in the pathway to London.

Margaret Brown said that people thought it was a stupid place to put the searchlight as it lit up the gasworks and made them a target.

Vic Foster was told that during the war, his shop – the butcher's in Vesta Avenue – remained empty after it was built and that the troops who were responsible for that area were billeted in his shop. There were no windows in it at the time. Margaret Brown says that one of the shops in Cottonmill Lane was taken over by the ARP.

There was an underground shelter in the school playing fields close to the path on Belmont Hill. According to John Buckingham, it was huge. He says the water table was very high in the playing fields and the shelter often had to be pumped out. Bill Mackenzie said that there must have been an air raid shelter in Cottonmill Lane (although Betty Cutler who lived opposite Bill cannot remember it). Bill played in the building after the war and his daughter-in-law, who has an allotment in the lane, has found several relics:

There was one there, an old ARP sign. When I said to her about the air-raid shelter she said it had probably been buried where they demolished it. She has it hanging up on her wall in her garden.

Where the maisonettes are at the end of Tavistock Avenue there was an air-raid siren. Tom Edgar described it as having a tripod of legs like telegraph poles with a platform on the top where the siren was situated. There was no air-raid shelter nearby so residents had to dive under the kitchen table when the siren went off.

Betty Cutler said that although there were a few bombs dropped around, where they were living in Cottonmill Crescent there was no real damage. A bomb did fall in Ramsbury Road in September 1940 which caused slight damage to a roof.[112] On the same night another landed on the golf course. Bombs also fell in Prospect Road and on the allotments in Cottonmill Lane.[113] Although there was slight damage to property, fortunately, there were no casualties. In November 1940, a high explosive bomb was dropped on the watercress beds. No one is sure on whose watercress beds the bomb fell: Pinnock's or Lee's. Wicker baskets used for storage and transport of produce were destroyed by the fire as were some trolleys and wagons which took produce to the local railway station.

Margaret Wickens said that during the early part of the war, when she was at St Peter's School, she never worried much about air raids as the family lived so close to the school:

Although we did have a scare in 1940 when Dad was on duty at Napsbury when a landmine dropped on the hospital.

Margaret Brown has some vivid memories:

When the bomb dropped at de Havilland's I was at school at Beaumont and we had to be in the shelters all day. When it was D-Day or Arnhem, the sky was black with the aeroplanes. There were gliders and all. The big Halifax bombers from Handley Page used to come back after bombing very low and they used to nearly hit the roofs. Little did I know I would end up working there, at Handley Page's. One night it was crashing and banging – because we used to hear it all from London – and you could see the sky lit up and then the planes [came] over, I think it must have been when they dropped . . . their load coming back, and I said Mum, can you hear that and my brother used to complain about me wailing and then one night the cats were howling outside and my brother threatened to put me outside with the cats!

Margaret Wickens' mother was always helping people. She was the one who collected money when a neighbour suffered a bereavement. She encouraged Margaret, even though she wasn't very old, to run a bazaar in the scout hut grounds in Old London Road where she raised the vast sum of £20 towards the Red Cross and had her picture in the *Herts Advertiser*. Margaret recalls many other childhood memories:

Apart from the wartime fundraising other memories include black-berrying and mushrooming in Cottonmill Lane before the housing estate was built, rosehip collecting for the national production of rosehip syrup, and elderberry collecting for Mum to dry and use in the place of currants to help out the rations. My mother was an excellent cook and always produced interesting meals from whatever was available. She also made all her own preserves, despite rationing, with whatever she could. My granddad kept his own chickens and a supply of eggs from these was a good supplement for national dried egg.

Right:
VE day party Leyland Avenue 1945 Courtesy John Buckingham

Other things I remember are: meeting my friend for play and collecting our El Dorado ice-cream from the factory in Cornwall Road – triangular ones in cardboard which you sucked from rather than licked; collecting jam jars for the war effort and taking them to Josh Pearce's scrap yard in my dolls pram, also newspapers; my grandfather making me a boat which sank when I took it to the lake at Verulamium; taking the accumulators for recharging for our radio which had replaced the crystal set; and being paid a penny or two from the neighbours for taking theirs; learning the Lambeth Walk from our neighbours who were billeted there; collecting wool from the barbed wire fence at the golf course – where sheep were kept during the war – for spinning lessons at school.

VE day party
Tavistock Avenue
1945
Courtesy
Tom Edgar

During the war, Margaret Wickens said there was a military outfit producing rubber on the lower part of the golf course. They pumped out some by-product which became a white pool of water. She paddled in it once and her mother was very cross.

There were many soldiers billeted in the town. Kathy Sinfield remembers the army coming to Doggetts Way:

When the war came, I was still at St Peter's School but in Doggetts Way the army had arrived. This was before the barracks were built where Westminster Lodge is now. It was fully manned with always a soldier on guard. It was very early on in the war when they hadn't arranged any parking so the Bren gun carriers were parked all the way up Doggetts Way and down Wilshere Avenue. We thought it was great because they were all Scotchmen [sic]. We thought they were some foreigners. They had Tam o' Shanters, and I found out that they were the Seaforth Highlanders and then of course the barracks were extended.

The Seaforth Highlanders left and the barracks were occupied by soldiers from the American army. Kathy Sinfield:

The GIs were all down there. In Watling Street – the bit that goes down near St Bart's Church – the small road leading off. The houses there were the accommodation for the American officers when they came. They were fairly new houses. I knew one man who bought one of the houses and everything in the house was painted dark green . . .

Kathy also remembers the evacuees:

When the soldiers moved out of the street that was the time the evacuees came down from London. So the people who had had the spare accommodation in Doggetts Way and Vesta Avenue, [first] had the soldiers billeted with them, [then] they had evacuees . . .

When I left St Peter's I went to Priory Park School which was next door and ... that was the time the evacuees came down from London ... The ones we had came from Ore just outside Hastings and it was the Ore School that moved in with us, the girls ... The schoolteacher who came with the Ore School, her name was Miss Freed and [she] became the first headmistress of St Julian's School. She stopped here as did several of them. I knew a couple of them who worked for Marks and Spencer's.

Everyone was rationed. Betty Cutler's father, who worked at Cell Barnes Hospital, managed to get extra sugar and meat so they fared pretty well. Many people supplemented the war rations by keeping pigs and chickens. Gerry Dunham remembers that his family and several others kept pigs on the allotments during the war and after. He said that a fellow called Les Clarke also had chickens and he even had a pony down there. Keeping pigs, he said, was like having a savings account:

> They bought them as baby pigs and reared them and when you sold them you had like a bank cheque from what you had been saving. They would collect them in cattle trucks and they would be taken to the slaughterhouse and turned into Walls pork sausages ...

Kathy Sinfield also remembers that the gasworks formed its own pig club with about three or four pigs:

> ... they reared [them] at the back in Doggetts field where the line of poplar trees is. There were allotments there then. There were always allotments and they [the allotment holders] used to take it in turn to feed the pigs and would collect swill. When the pigs were slaughtered, then everybody in the club got part of the pig, which helped with the rationing.

Kathy also remembers a Mr Hill who came round on his cart selling freshly caught rabbit:

> and then he'd buy the skin back off of you for sixpence.

Gerry Dunham said that he was a scrounger during the war. He often used to scrounge food off people. He remembers Mrs Ridley at the Sunday school. She used to give them a drink and some bread and jam before they left. He also went round to a man called Clarke in Old London Road to go shopping for food for him.

The Vickers Armstrong experimental tank which sits between the golf course and the London Road station, now Orient Close, played a big part in the war. Many residents say that they used the tank to practise bouncing the 'bombs' which were eventually used for real to destroy the Mohne Dam in the Ruhr Valley. Bill Mackenzie remembers that there was a storm drain that came from Bucknall's Drive in Bricket Wood where there was a replica model of the Mohne Dam and they put a little bit of explosive in, just to make enough of a hole in the wall to flood the 'Ruhr Valley'.

> So they damned the storm drain up, built this replica dam, let the water come down so it filled up. They got little bits of explosive until there was a hole big enough to blow out so that the water came over and carried on there, and they worked out from that how much explosive they would need to blow up the Mohne Dam.

Bill was once taken on a visit to the Vickers Armstrong tank building where there was a model of a trawler in the tank:

> This bloke – he may have just been the caretaker, I don't know – he simulated a storm for us and calm water and everything. We watched this trawler go in the tank. They could simulate storms and all sorts in this tank. They had massive fans going.

Roy Buckingham, a respected cousin of John Buckingham and a hero of his, was born in Sopwell in 1923 in the Railway Cottages on Holywell Hill. Roy played an important part in the war. Although he was underage, he applied to join the RAF. He was working for Mercer Chronometers at the time and his manager threatened him with the sack if he went for an interview. Eventually, he was accepted by the RAF and trained as a pilot/navigator. Much of his flying was in secret and involved dropping supplies and equipment to the Resistance in France and Belgium and later in Norway. He was with the 138 squadron. His neighbours were unaware of his war involvement and some of them despised him for supposedly not joining in the war effort.

Tavistock Avenue
VE Day celebrations
Courtesy St Albans
Museum

He used to love going to Norway, going over frozen countryside and just looking down obviously deciding if the lights and things were in the right place to drop his supplies. He showed me all of his false papers . . . they used to drop bicycles . . . but the brave part to me was going down to France and working with the Resistance. He used to say that even the people on the base were never sure where they were going . . . He did about two years in that and then he went back . . . That was a volunteer squadron, he was asked to volunteer. In other words . . . in air force terms it was more like you, you and you. Then he went back . . . at the end of the war going back on the bombing raids. After the war, he carried on in the RAF and he was doing mapping of Europe . . . taking photographs of Europe.

While in training overseas, Roy wrote an evocative poem to his mother which was read out at his funeral in December 2011. It describes his boyhood home in Sopwell in the second stanza: the river and the watermill and the 'quaint old church' which is St Stephen's.

<u>Homeland</u>

Although an ocean doth divide
And keep me from your loving side
I know your love is ever near
Protecting me from every fear
For though in foreign lands I roam,
My heart is really always home,
And though I fly o'er wind-swept plains,
I long to see those English lanes
Anew and blooming in the Spring
In England where the thrushes sing.

Those lands of mine I know so well
Those woods where grows the sweet bluebell,
Those fields so old yet ever new,
That home where I in boyhood grew,
That quaint old church upon the hill,
That river and the water mill,
They're English 'neath an English sky,
They're yours, and mine, until we die
So though I'm far across the sea
That England's still a part of me.

When the war was over, there were many street parties to celebrate Victory in Europe Day. Tavistock Avenue and Leyland Avenue had parties which were featured in the *Herts Advertiser*.

Kathy Sinfield remembers the soldiers returning:

The soldiers were just coming out after the war having been demobbed and when they had signed on they used to have letters after their name to indicate what they were and if you had a B after your name you were a builder and they were the first ones to come out of the army to build the houses and they started on Cottonmill Lane.

Coronation day Leyland Avenue 1953
Courtesy John Buckingham

Chapter Six
The rise of the post-war estates

As part of the post-war housing boom, the Cottonmill and St Julian's housing estates began to grow. Where once there were footpaths and fields, now there were roads and houses. Berners Drive, Priory Walk, Monks Close and Abbots Avenue were among the first roads to be built between 1946 and 1948 and houses were built on both sides of Cottonmill Lane. Next came Nuns Lane and Gorham Drive and Butterfield Lane. Some of the houses in Nuns Lane were built specifically for Naval officers. The Cottonmill estate stopped at the top of Abbots Avenue by the railway line. Above the railway was still all farmland until well after the war when they started building the prefabs and then the houses. Nancy Broadbent's sister remembers going with her father and picking mushrooms in the fields around this area. The houses in Creighton Avenue were not built until 1952 and those in Maynard Drive were built in 1956.

Street names

Some enterprising council employees at one time decided that the names of the roads on the estates should reflect people who once lived in the area. Hence we have several roads with connections to the abbey and the monasteries, and in particular, Sopwell Nunnery: Priory Walk, Abbots Avenue, Monks Close, Monks Gate, Nunnery Close, Nunnery Stables, Nuns Lane, Old Sopwell Gardens, Martyr Close, Cloister Garth, Deacon Close. Berners Drive is named after Juliana Berners who may have been a prioress at the nunnery and said to be the author of the *Boke of St Albans*.

Many of the streets are named after abbots:
- Gorham Drive is named after Abbot Geoffrey de Gorham. The name Gorham comes from Gorram Castle in France. Geoffrey, the abbot for 36 years, is said to have founded many cells or small religious houses that remained under the protection of the Abbey: Sopwell Priory, St Julian's leper hospital, Cell Barnes and St Mary of the Prae.
- Mentmore Drive is named after Michael de Mentmore who was abbot from 1336 to 1349.
- Wallingford Walk is named after Richard of Wallingford (1292–1336). He was a mathematician who made major contributions to astronomy/astrology and horology while serving as Abbot of St Albans Abbey. There was also a William Wallingford, the 36th abbot.
- Trumpington Drive is named after William de Trumpington, the 22nd abbot.
- Ramryge Court is named after Thomas Ramryge, the 37th abbot.
- Kempe Close may have been named after David Kempe, Archdeacon of St Albans 1560–1581.

Then there are the Richard Lee connections:
- Sadleir Road: Sir Ralph Sadleir married Ann, the daughter of Richard Lee.
- Coningsby Bank is named after Maud Coningsby, Lee's other daughter.
- There used to be a Lee Lane. It was a road leading off Holyrood Crescent opposite Creighton Avenue where the flats are now. The houses in Lee Lane were prefabricated.

Other well known people with local connections had streets named after them:
- Grindcobbe is named after William Grindcobbe who was one of the leaders killed in the Peasants' Revolt and was subsequently seen as a martyr.
- De Tany Court, Albeny Gate and Henrys Grant: Richard de Tany and Henry de Albini both gave grants of land to Sopwell Priory. This is also where Henry's Grant comes from. De Albini is most likely the origin of Albeny Gate.
- Mercers Row is named after Thomas Mercer who had his factory in Prospect Road and then Eywood Road.
- Butterfield Lane is named after George Butterfield. Father and son, both named George, were millers in Sopwell Mill in Cottonmill Lane.
- Holyrood Crescent and Lectern Lane were named after the eagle lectern (Holyrood bird) in St Stephen's Church.
- Creighton Avenue is named after George Creichton, Bishop of Dunkeld, who was the abbot at Holyrood.
- Boleyn Drive is named after Anne Boleyn.
- Mandeville Drive is probably named after Sir John Mandeville, a fourteenth-century knight who compiled a singular book of supposed travels. He was reputedly born in St Albans.
- Mitchell Close: It is believed that the name Mitchell originates from the designer of the Spitfire/Hurricane, R.J. Mitchell, although it could be after Abe Mitchell, the golfer depicted on the Ryder Cup.

However, there are still many street names the provenance of which remain totally obscure.

The prefabs and early houses

Many of the first houses were prefabricated, and so were easy and quick to assemble. There is a report in the *Herts Advertiser* in August 1948 of fifty aluminium bungalows having been erected on the St Julian's estate, and that fifty more were expected in another month.[114] The bungalows were clad in aluminium sheeting with aluminium frames using recovered metal from scrapped planes from the war. The first fifty were erected on Lectern Lane, Holyrood Crescent and Creighton Avenue and they only took 20–30 minutes to erect. The prefabs arrived in four pieces complete with fittings. These bungalows were described as Hawkesley's aluminium dwellings which were

> very pleasantly situated on a slope affording an uninterrupted view of St Albans.

They were placed in three rows following the contours of the hill from north-east to south-west with a fourth block from north to south and were described as being of a permanent type of bungalow with an estimated life of sixty years and ideal for a family of three or four. The prefabs which are still in Mitchell Close are of this type of dwelling and have proved that they are long lasting. The provision of these aluminium bungalows had ceased by October 1948. However, the other smaller prefabs continued to be built. Bill Mackenzie can remember big lorries with half a prefab on each coming along Cottonmill Lane. They were put together within a day.

There were also prefabs in Tavistock Avenue, where Tavistock Close is now, and in Berners Drive and Watling View. These can be seen in the aerial photograph opposite. Many people have fond memories of the prefabs which came with many modern conveniences and were very cosy. The kitchen had a sink, gas stove, gas boiler, fitted units (complete with mop and broom cupboard), table and even a fridge. The bathroom (including indoor toilet) came with a towel rail, mirror and cupboard and the bedrooms had fitted wardrobes. They had small Nissen hut type sheds in their back gardens.

By October 1948, the council had 506 completed and occupied houses, both permanent and temporary, which had been built since the end of the war. Many of these were in Cottonmill. To celebrate the completion of the five hundredth house, the mayor held a sherry party and invited the five hundredth tenant, Mr and Mrs Leslie Lane of 50 Nuns Lane, to receive the keys to their house at the ceremony.[115]

The roads were originally built of concrete with black asphalt lines joining each section. On the aerial maps they stand out because they are so white. This surface made them very bumpy but in those days there were fewer cars. Tarmac came a lot later. Originally there were no pavements, just mud tracks with the boundaries of the properties marked with wire.[116]

Joan Forder:

> I remember all the houses going up and we used to go in them. They were all empty. There was nobody there at night so we used to have a wander round. I would have been thirteen.

Berners Drive, on the Cottonmill side was completed in 1948. Pam Marshall gives an evocative description of what it was like at the time:

> My family moved to our new council house in Berners Drive on the Cottonmill estate in the autumn of 1948. I was five years old and at infant school then. My house was in the middle of Berners Drive. Berners Drive is next to the railway bank. There were two lots of four houses with Georgian houses on the end. If you go down Berners Drive there is a dip and my house was there. When we moved in they were still building along Cottonmill Lane. Our new home was a semi-detached brick built building, with Georgian windows, and a Georgian front door. There were three bedrooms, a bathroom, kitchen with a back door leading into the garden, a front room and a dining room. We had a front, side and a large back garden. In the back garden were two brick built sheds. Our garden backed on to the gardens in Cottonmill Lane, and between the houses we had a lovely view of the golf links. The house seemed enormous to us, and my dad was so pleased to have a big garden as well. We kept poultry and grew all our own vegetables. We had good and friendly neighbours and it grew into a lovely community. When I was a child, Berners Drive consisted of houses down one side only, with a green strip on the other. At the rear of the strip of grass were bushes, and through the bushes was the railway bank. At the bottom of Berners Drive, just past Priory Walk, was a footpath that divided

into two, the left path went over the railway line as a level crossing, and the right path led up to the bridge. This path had a sign saying 'Cycling Prohibited', so that was what we called it. St Julian's estate across the bridge at Abbots Avenue West did not exist then. There were no shops, churches, no buses, or schools. We walked all the way to Alma Road School each day. We had to go over the bridge at the bottom end of Berners Drive to the nearest shops which were in Cottonmill Lane.

Lil Day says that the houses in Priory Walk and other nearby roads were the envy of other council tenants because of their position:

When we first came here, no end of people wanted to come here because it had such a beautiful outlook. There were no trees there then. From the windows you could see all over the golf course and the trains going along. It was such a good view. You could see the Abbey from the garden. Lots of people used to say, oh I would love to live there – do you want to exchange? . . . A lady came to live here who came from Wilshere Avenue and her house had been pulled down because the council were building a road through to build flats in Praetorian Court. The lady had turned down a couple of houses [before she went to Cottonmill] and made all sorts of demands on the council before she would accept it, including a run in for a car and skirting boards because there were no skirting boards in these houses then. Everything she wanted she got. She wanted the loft insulated and she got that done long before any of us had it. She got all that plus money to move in.

Vic Foster, who moved to one of the first houses to be built in Cottonmill Lane, number 58, remembers that there were no roads then, just the tracks. The corner houses were built first and occupied. The rest were built while his family were living there. He remembers there being a night watchman on site, for security purposes, who chewed tobacco and spat.

Doggetts Way, Wilshere Avenue, Tavistock Avenue and Vesta Avenue 15.3.1949 © English Heritage. (NMR) RAF Photography

Bobby Jones lived in Butterfield Lane from the late sixties until the mid seventies:

The houses in Butterfield Lane were Airey houses built by prisoners of war. They were only meant to last thirty years but people bought them but then the council had to buy them back because they had defects. They had to be reinforced because the iron girders had rusted. They were built just after the war like the prefabs.

There were strict rules attached to being a council tenant. For example, tenants were only allowed one animal and gardens had to be maintained. The rent man who came round regularly to collect the rent would report any abuse of the rules. Even so, there appeared to be a lot of anti-social behaviour. At a meeting of the council in November 1951, several members objected to the proposal to spend £1,300 on trees and the installation of oak posts to prevent cars being parked on the edges of the green spaces in the Cottonmill and St Julian's estates. The reason for their objection was that trees had been planted before and had been wantonly destroyed by residents. Residents had apparently been sent a circular letter about the havoc which was being caused by this wanton destruction and there had been no evidence to suggest that their behaviour had improved since then. Despite these objections, the scheme was approved and the trees were planted along the grass verges and in front gardens.[117]

It must be said that the residents of the new estates, unsettled by the war, took several years to form into a community. Unfortunately, on the way, there are many tales of anti-social behaviour and vandalism in Sopwell.

Prefabs in Mitchell Close © Sandy Norman

Eventually, the council pulled down most of the prefabs and replaced them with houses. However, the fact that tenants were very reluctant to leave the prefabs is an indicator of the quality and popularity of that type of housing at the time. Bill Mackenzie remembers that some of them were still there until the 1960s, and the ones in Mitchell Close survive to this day. The council proposed demolishing the Mitchell Close prefabs in 1980 but the tenants set up a petition and were successful in persuading the council to change their minds. They still look very well kept. Many of them have been purchased from the council.

There was a house in Nuns Lane that was struck by lightning in the early 1950s. Vera Foster lived in Cottonmill Lane at the time. Their house overlooked the golf course and the family were in the kitchen when it happened:

There was no thunder or lightning but suddenly this big ball of fire came across from the golf course and round to the back and there was this almighty bang and we went out into Cottonmill Lane and stood opposite Nuns Lane and it had hit a house in Nuns Lane. The family had to be moved out. The same house was hit again sometime later.

The first house on the right-hand corner of Abbots Avenue West and Holyrood Crescent was a doctor's surgery and the doctor was called Doctor Ingelby. The house is still there although the surgery is long gone. Doctor Ingelby also had a surgery in Watling Street opposite St Julian's School. Vic Foster says the posh clients went to the Watling Street surgery while the council tenants went to the rough one. The doctor was well liked but a bit of a drinker and often had the shakes. Vic Foster describes him as looking like Charlie Chaplin but without the bowler hat.

Fancy dress party in Pemberton Close June 1953 Courtesy Bobby Jones

Roads, bridges and transport

The shape of Cottonmill Lane changed after the war when Berners Drive and Priory Walk were being constructed. The road did not have such a sharp bend round to the left after the railway bridge, but continued straight to approximately where Priory Walk meets Berners Drive. It then bent to the left following what was to become Priory Walk, and then straightened up. The new form of the road was built with rubble from the bombing of London which was brought in on lorries and tipped down the banks. Many residents report that the rubble was quite fancy, not just old bricks.

John Buckingham remembers the workmen demolishing the railway bridge which used be just a single cart track with just one arch:

... they dumped, smashed down [the arch] and ... they brought in the beams on the Watford line, big concrete beams and they brought in a steam crane, a railway steam crane this was and it was the biggest engine in my memory – 2.8.0 Stanier – a big freight engine ... They backed it along and put the crane in the right position, they picked the beams up and swung them up onto the bridge ...

Margaret Brown:

They built the road from rubble from London and built it up high then cut the road across the field. At the back of these houses there was a field that went right through to Priory Walk as it is now and then the road came along Priory Walk.

Bill Mackenzie:

Because Cottonmill Lane itself, [when] you come over the railway bridge and then [the road] goes round to the left but I think at one stage it must have gone straight down because I can remember that hill being built. It was all built from brick rubble from London from the bombing. They brought all that brick rubble out to build up there.

Kathy Sinfield:

When the war ended, the boys came back and the first houses that were built were just over the bridge in Cottonmill Lane and they built the wide serviceable road then and the rubble that was the hard core of the road was the rubble brought from London from the buildings that had all been bombed. They were clearing London.

Joan Forder:

Because [Cottonmill Lane] went right across the fields didn't it. [It] used to go over the bridge and then just round and then they built the road across. That was all fields there and I used to see it getting higher and higher as they put the road on the top. Lorry after lorry used to come down and tip. We used to play on there and then they built the road on top of it. Because living in Boleyn Drive, when you used to look out of the bedroom window, you could just watch them doing it. There was nothing there, only the railway, and we looked over the railway – the Hatfield line – and you could see the lorries just coming down and tipping it all. It makes you wonder really what's under that road because when they picked the rubble up there were bits of houses and some of their bits of furniture.

Pamela Marshall:

Between Berners Drive and the path was waste land, with a very steep bank up to Cottonmill Lane as it curved round and up over the bridge. Lorries would reverse here, and dump soil down the bank. We all loved playing on the banks and finding lumps of chalk and bits of slate amongst the debris. It was great for playing hopscotch etc. . . . as we had pavement slabs.

In 1948, the council tried to get a bus service installed on the Cottonmill estate but the London Transport Executive said they were unable to do so because of the state of the roads leading to the estate. Cyril Dumpleton, the MP at the time, also got involved, saying it was important for the schoolchildren to have a bus service.[118] One of the problems was the railway bridge in what was to be Abbots Avenue.

Margaret Brown:

You couldn't get through into St Julian's because you couldn't go over the bridge – it was only a cattle bridge. Even when they first built the estate, it was still a cattle bridge. Then they reinforced the bridge and then the bus used to go there. When the bus service first started, it used to be circular. It would go down Prospect Road but then they stopped that when they put the road humps in. So now they have to have two buses. After you got over that cattle bridge it was fields for a long time then they built St Julian's.

Vic Foster remembers some time in the early 1950s a double-decker bus losing control on an icy Abbots Avenue. It had been raining and the concrete surface had frozen.

The bus came downhill from the King Offa down the dual carriageway and it went straight into the wall of the flats opposite the dual carriageway in Cottonmill Lane. It flattened the wall. In those days, the bus went down one side of the dual carriageway and turned round and came up again because the bridge over the river at Cottonmill [by the swimming baths] was not strong enough. The bridge was strengthened when they straightened out the bend.

In those days the 325 bus went from the Cottonmill estate all the way to Townsend.

In 1950, Pemberton Close, Mandeville Drive, Trumpington Drive and the east end of Maynard Drive were built. Pemberton Close, along with many other roads had street parties when Queen Elizabeth II was crowned on 2nd June 1953.

Bobby Jones lived in Pemberton Close:

Maynard Drive was a building site. The Trumpington end was already there. We used to go and play in the empty houses that were under construction. It was a long time after before they built up the rest of Maynards. The left-hand side of the road coming from Pemberton was just grass as we used to cross it to go to the shops in Vesta . . . The area of green behind Pemberton [is where] they used to have a communal bonfire night.

Coronation day
Pemberton Close
June 1953
Courtesy
Lee Welch

Schools and churches

St Peter's School in Cottonmill Lane is by far the oldest school in Sopwell. It started off as two schools, a church school for boys and girls over seven and a school for infants from two to seven. The building was situated originally on Old London Road where the Priory Park complex is now. It was built between 1850 and 1851 on land granted by the Earl of Verulam. The foundation stone was laid by Elizabeth Joanna, Countess of Verulam on 12th November 1850.

St Peter's infants school occupied one large room at the west of the old building. The church school for juniors was in an adjacent room about 40 feet by 20 feet. Both schools opened on 29th September 1851 and soon had 120 and 160 children on the registers.[119] The staff in each school consisted of a mistress assisted by pupil teachers and monitors. A child could become a pupil teacher at the age of thirteen, and receive tuition from her mistress while teaching for a maximum of 25 hours per week. Children served a five-year apprenticeship as a pupil teacher. In 1872, there were about 130 infants in the one room without dividing partitions or curtains.

Boys in the church school were transferred to Christ Church School in Verulam Road in January 1893. Later on, in 1901, another school was built for the senior pupils. Called Priory Park, it was built alongside the eastern end of St Peter's. St Peter's later became a Church of England primary school and Priory Park became a senior girls' school.[120] The senior boys went to the school in Hatfield Road in the old Pemberton building.

St Peter's ceased to be a Church of England school

Right:
Book awarded to Grace Butterfield of St Peter's school in 1909 Courtesy Margaret Wickens

Grace Butterfield
Prize for
General Thoughtfulness
&
Good Conduct
given by
Miss Crowdy

St Peter's Girls' School
St Albans.

Dec: 1909.

after the Second World War and became a County Primary. In 1953, St Peter's took over the Priory Park building when the girls from that school together with the boys from Hatfield Road School were transferred to the new St Julian's secondary school (later renamed Marlborough) in Watling Street.

The land on which the present school is situated was allotments until well after the war. The site was acquired in 1968 and the school moved into the present building in Cottonmill Lane on 31st January 1975; the new nursery department opened on Monday 3rd February 1975.[121]

When the school first started, education had to be paid for. In 1882, the charge per pupil per week was fourpence (boys), threepence (girls) and twopence (infants). The (head)mistress was Miss Gifford assisted by three pupil teachers, an infant schoolmistress (Miss Hunter) plus two more pupil teachers and an assistant. The average attendance was 204.[122]

Kathy Sinfield went to St Peter's School:

> ... and being a Church of England school it was connected with St Peter's. On church holidays like Ash Wednesday we would go in a crocodile down Old London Road and up the hill to St John's Church at the top of Old London Road about opposite Alma Road.

Betty Cutler says that on Mondays the girls from Priory Park went to the Art School for cooking, laundry and science. Margaret Wickens attended St Peter's between 1937 and 1943. Her parents were also pupils at one time. Margaret remembers some of her teachers: Miss Hodges, Miss Tight, Miss Brinklow and Miss Bunfield.

> Miss Hornblower was headmistress until she retired and Miss Bunfield took over. I kept in touch with Miss Brinklow after she married (Mrs Burrows) and Miss Bunfield until two years after I was married in 1958.

Vic Foster went to St Peter's in the 1940s and he remembers some of the teachers: Miss Norris, Mr Stickland and the headmistress, Miss Bunfield. Later Mr Stickland became

Priory Park
girls c.1940s
Courtesy
Kathy
Sinfield

headmaster. John Buckingham has fond memories of the school, when aged five or six. His first teacher was a Mrs Irmston:

> In her classroom there were all these grey cupboards. The small cupboard round the top were full of toys. We were always promised if we were good children that the doors would be open and we would have the toys out – but we never did . . . From starting at school we'd moved up and we had another teacher, Miss Smith, I remember her as clear as if it was yesterday . . . She was a fairly new teacher but she was OK, firm and fair. Mrs Hodgkins was a caring lovely teacher and then we went on to Mr Rawlings, our first man teacher and he was very understanding . . . I learnt a lot from him . . . [I] was envious [of] the girls . . . in Priory Park. Because Priory Park School was part of the school which is in Old London Road which was a girls school . . . And they used to come in a lorry for these girls and pick them up to go potato picking and I was so envious as I would much rather have gone potato picking . . . I think it was Fridays we used to go off to play football at Cunningham Hill . . . and we didn't have coaches to pick us up – our little legs – we used to have to walk . . .

St Peter's school (Priory Park building) before conversion to Old Priory Park housing development. © John Buckingham

Mandeville JMI School was built in 1950 and opened on 8th January 1951. Council minutes at the time stated that the school was

> intended to serve the new Cottonmill estate which when complete will have 716 houses. At present 656 houses are occupied and there will be a further 60 to be finished during 1951. A new JMI school, Mandeville, to accommodate 320 pupils is being opened on the estate in January 1951.

The first head teacher was Miss Knight. Miss Knight kept a school log from the first day until she retired in 1970. Her entry for the very first day said that they had 263 pupils but by October 1954 there were 384 pupils which was far higher than the 320 originally planned. The members of staff in 1951 were: Miss A.H. Knight, Mr F. James, Mr R. Meyrick, Mr T.S. Collins, Miss D. Blower, Mrs Bridges, Miss J. Winchester, Miss S. Tatchell and Mrs M.E. Nichols. Mr James didn't have a very good start. On the second day, he slipped on the ice and damaged his back and was off sick for three weeks.

The first meeting of the parent teacher association was in March 1952. Miss Knight was the chairman, Mr Meyrick was the vice-chairman, Mr F. Jones was the treasurer, and the secretary was Mr E.J. Penikett. The other members were: Mrs S. A. Tatchell, Mrs A.M. Pope, Mrs E. Williams, Mr W.D. Busby and Mr A.E. Fieber.

In 1953, just before the Queen's coronation, there was a service of thanksgiving to wish the Queen well and each child was given a coronation beaker to commemorate the event. In 1964 there was an entry in the log of a harvest festival where fruit and vegetables were given to Vesta Lodge and Sopwell House old people's homes. In 1966 the school acquired a television set. In November 1969, some of the staff took industrial action because of low salaries.

The school had a very relaxed atmosphere in the 1970s. The children were allowed to call some of their teachers by their first names. The head teacher then was Frank Miles. Some of the names remembered by residents are: Mrs Williams, Eve Harper, Pam Strowman, Hazel Webber, Cynthia Trotman, Irene Fernandez, Deirdre Walker, Moyra Brown, George Bell and Mrs Osborn. Mr Miles also kept a school log and reported in 1973 that ten traveller children were admitted to the school from a nearby site and that some of them had severe social problems. Mr Stuart Stonehouse took over as head teacher in 1980. In 1996, Michael Howard visited the school. The present head is Amanda Godfrey. Today, the school is much larger, having recently been extended.

Bobby Jones was one of Mandeville's first pupils:

> I started off at St Peter's because Mandeville wasn't built. I can remember us all being in the hall while they sorted out the classes. I remember Miss Knight the headmistress. She was tall and large with a port wine birthmark on her neck. I remember a Mr Bridges who came from St Peter's.

Nancy Broadbent started at Mandeville in 1954. She remembers Mrs Burrell who taught the infants and Mrs Beere and Miss Thorpe; and the dinner ladies were Miss French and Mrs Wilson.

> We did some lovely things at Mandeville. We used to have the little fairs and that sort of thing, dancing and the usual things. We used to have assemblies in those days, proper assemblies when you all sing and say prayers.

John Buckingham belonged to a men's club which met at the school:

> I was involved in another club which was in Mandeville School. We had a men's club up there which I got pushed into at a young age, in my early twenties I think it was, to be a chairman . . . it used to be Bill Clarke before me . . . We played snooker and table tennis, cards, dominoes, had a chat and a cup of tea, a good friendly club.

St Adrian's School, in Watling View, was opened in 1960. However the opening ceremony was not held until the following year. Its 50th anniversary was in 2010. The school held a special open day, having collected memorabilia from past pupils and staff including many old photographs and uniforms. There were displays showing themes or events from the 1960s which were made by the children, and among the guests were eight former pupils from the very first class at the school.

St Adrian's school staff 1963 Courtesy St Adrian's school

More than 550 people turned out for the school's jubilee mass in the week after which was celebrated by the Most Revd Vincent Nichols, Archbishop of Westminster. Other dignitaries in attendance included St Albans Mayor, Cllr Maxine Crawley. The service was followed by a reception in a marquee which included a buffet. Fifty balloons were released to mark the occasion.

In 1963, Irene Ewer went to St Adrian's. Mother Edith was the head teacher. Irene says that the staff were very strict. She liked Sister Mary Paul who taught her in year one:

> . . . she was a lovely lady All the teachers were nuns of course, apart from one man: Mr Malaney. The nuns dressed in full habits with heavy rosary beads around their necks and were sometimes intimidating. Mr Collett was the caretaker. All the children had to go to St Bart's for mass which they never understood as it was always in Latin.

Watling View School is a state community special school for children and young people with severe learning difficulties. They take children of both genders aged two to nineteen, mainly from St Albans and the surrounding area. It was opened in the late 1960s.

St Julian's Church, situated in Abbots Avenue has an interesting history. After the war, many newly housed residents on the Cottonmill and St Julian's estates wanted somewhere to worship. In 1948, permission was granted for the use of a converted Nissen hut in Cottonmill Lane as a Sunday school. This was an old wartime hut which had stood in fields as part of an anti-aircraft searchlight emplacement. On 1st December 1951 there was a service of dedication for the new temporary church of St Julian. Present at the dedication service were: the Revd George Byrne (the priest-in-charge of St Julian's housing estate), the Bishop of St Albans, Revd A. McInness, the mayor (R.G. Thompson), Canon A.F.S. Harding (Vicar of St Stephen's) and Canon F.G. Brenchley.[123]

The present building dates from 1956, and was partly paid for by individual community subscriptions of sixpence. The church was built as a daughter church, to be the responsibility of St Stephen's. In practice, however, St Julian's largely runs its own affairs.[124] An extension to the church was completed in the spring of 2010 and was formally opened by Bishop Alan.

Lil Day remembers collecting money to build St Julian's Church:

> I had an old lady I was looking after and Reverend Folland, used to give her communion in the front room and he said to me about going round collecting for the church. I went all the way down Cottonmill and all the way back.

John Buckingham remembers a man called Bill Clarke who ran a table tennis club in the church in the 1960s:

> He was a great man, good with people of all ages.

Pamela Marshall can remember St Julian's Church being blessed by the bishop. She said the Nissen hut was at the back of where the car park of the church is now:

> . . . and that's where we used to do our jiving on a Wednesday. The vicar used to let us have it and someone would bring along a record player and some records. The Nissen hut was the original church.

There is another church on the opposite side of Abbots Avenue which is run by the **Christadelphians.** This church started life as a Baptist church and was staffed by teachers from the Dagnall Street and Tabernacle Baptist churches. As with St Julian's Church, the money to build the church came from the community. In January 1952, the Cottonmill Baptist Sunday school held its annual promotion service in Mandeville School which was conducted by 'Uncle Mac' (Mr N.D. MacLeod) the superintendent.[125] In May 1952, the church held its first sale of work at Mandeville School.[126] The *Herts Advertiser* for 6th June 1952 states:

Yet another licence has been obtained for the erection of a building on the Cottonmill estate where for some time the two churches: Dagnall Street and the Tabernacle, had been jointly engaged in pioneering work. Here, as in some other districts, it is among children and women that greater response was forthcoming. Workers from both these churches were giving their time and the strain was considerable. Now that a building had to be erected the strain would be financial.

In 1968, the Cottonmill Baptists merged with Park Street Baptists and the building was vacated. The premises were then sold to a housing association with planning permission to build six flats or two pairs of semi-detached houses. The money was never raised so this did not happen. The building was left vacant until June 1976 when it came up for auction and was bought by the Christadelphian church. By that time the building was in a very poor state and the roof leaked. Members of the church set to and repaired and extended the building and the grounds. They had to remove about 150 tons of fly-tipped rubbish from the car park.[127]

St Bartholomew's (Bart's) Roman Catholic Church is on the corner of Vesta Avenue and Watling Street. The church is thought to be situated on the land which was probably the church of the medieval leper hospital of St Julian. St Bart's was opened in 1964. The idea to build it came from Father Michael O'Learey and the Missionaries of the Sacred Heart at the mother church of St Alban and St Stephen. With the acceleration of post-war housing, Father O'Learey saw that there was a need for a parish and he bought land on which to build St Adrian's School and later for the church.[128] The first parish priest was Father Joseph Gardner. Irene Ewer remembers that he wore a monocle. The present incumbent is Father Tim Edgar.

Bill Mackenzie and his wife should have been one of the first couples to get married in St Bart's:

St Julian's Sunday school in the Vesta Avenue butchers in the 1940s Courtesy Vic Foster

Father Gardiner was the parish priest and we should have been the first couple to get married in St Bart's but they didn't get their licence in time so we got married down Beaconsfield Road. He was the first priest to go there. He didn't go down too well with a lot of people as he was an ex-padre from the army. He lived in a prefab. As you come up the hill – you just come over the brow of the hill and there used to be a little cutting big enough for a couple of cars to go in and he lived in a prefab in there.

While sorting jumble for a jumble sale at St Bart's, helpers found a Second World War mortar shell in a box. The Bomb Disposal Unit had to be called and they evacuated the immediate area. It was later taken away and all was safe.

St Julian's Sunday School was a little non-denominational Sunday school. It was situated in huts at the end of the footpath between Tavistock Avenue and Maynard Drive, Mandeville School end. This started life in the 1940s in the right-hand side of R. E. Holdham's butchers shop in Vesta Avenue. It was originally run by Miss L. Weldon. Nancy Broadbent's sister Valerie, attended. After a fundraising exercise, they moved to the huts in 1951. These were opened by the mayor, Mr R.G. Thompson. The butcher and former mayor, Mr Holdham, was presented with a golden key.[129] In 1951, an approach was made to Mandeville School from the *Tavistock* Sunday school to use Mandeville for some of their events so it appears to have acquired a new name.

Right:
St Julian's Sunday school 1953 Courtesy Lee Welch

In the 1960s and 1970s the Sunday school was run by Mr and Mrs Collins and Mrs Welch. Nancy Broadbent's children attended and remembers that it had a choir and an annual Rose Queen festival. It closed down when Mrs Collins retired and, unfortunately, it was subjected to two arson attacks and eventually had to be pulled down. Val Allen, living in Tavistock Avenue, saw both blazes. The firemen put the first fire out from her garden. The area where the Sunday school once stood now contains mobile homes.

A playgroup was also held in the huts, run by Mrs Collins. After she retired, it was run for a while by Mrs Mary Mower and Nancy Broadbent. This playgroup later relocated to St Bart's Church hall.

Shops

Most of the provisions were delivered until well after the war. The milk was delivered by horse and cart usually from the local farms. Old milk bottles have been found with Coaker Sopwell Mill Farm, W.G. Brown Sopwell Home Farm and Muir St Julian's Farm inscribed on them. Other shops had arrangements for delivering to their customers. Margaret Brown:

> There would be Shepherds the baker's down Old London Road, the greengrocer used to come round and of course the milkman (Co-op Dairy) and then there was Muir's [St Julian's Farm], he used to come round. The ordinary grocers, such as Home and Colonial used to deliver. You went in and put your order in and they delivered. Everyone used to go out to the van for the greengrocery. It used to be Pinnocks. There used to be a little butcher's up Alma Cut. He was a good butcher and my mum used to get her meat or order it from there . . . in Old London Road there used to be Caley's. My mother also used to have the hat people from Luton with boxes of hats to try them on. My mum worked in the hat factory in St Albans. It used to be quite an event because you would be there and your mum would be trying the hats on.

Vesta Avenue butcher shop, 1990s. © Vic Foster

Kathy Sinfield:

We still had the horse and cart delivering milk and vegetables. Mr Cotton used to come in his old boneshaker with the coal and Mr Shepherd used to come with the horse and cart with the bread. The bakery was in Old London Road.

Bill Mackenzie:

The Co-op used to have a mobile shop and it used to come round twice a week. He was a little bloke and used to have a little shop up Albert Street. He used to come round Saturdays. He was like a little grocer. That was all before the shops in Abbots Avenue. Pinnocks had a greengrocery in St Albans and when we first went down to Cottonmill, he used to come round. There were no shops then. [On] Saturdays they used to come round with a van selling greengroceries. They would knock on your door and ask you if you wanted anything. You had to get your greengroceries that way.

Lil Day has many memories of making ends meet:

When I first moved down here we used to have Kingsbury Mill's [milk]. Their depot was in Branch Road. There was a woman and she had a horse and cart and we had the milk in bottles. The greengrocer used to come round with the horse and cart. He was a local bloke. My meat – it was on rations still – came from Holdham's butcher's of Park Street. He used to come twice a week, a Wednesday and a Saturday. I used to have neck of mutton, or half a pig's head to make brawn on a Wednesday and it cost about one and six. At the weekend I would have a joint. When I first moved down here I used to get my groceries delivered from Park Street until I got used to the area and then I got them from down here . . . I had my shoes on tick from a chap called Mr Wray and he had a very old-fashioned van similar to those you see on the Brighton run and he lived in Alexander Road and he used to come down every week and bring brand new shoes and they were really strong shoes, leather, and we used to pay half a crown a week. He said, if you haven't got it don't worry. He said he just comes for the company. He used to go to quite a few of us round here. My kids always had good shoes on their feet and they were solid shoes. He was an old man and getting older and he said don't worry if there's still money on the book when I die all that money goes with me. He said my brother is not getting a penny of my money, my customers come first. And then there was another shop down Fleetville, a wool shop, and he used to come round and sell wool, knitting wool, Rainbow wool and they used to charge, I think, two shillings a week. I didn't knit, my girls used to use it. I used to do my own needlework, you see, I used to make the girls dresses. [Where did you get your material from then?] Jumble sales. When I went to jumble sales I would look at the dresses and find the material that I liked, if it was good material, and unpick it and cut the pattern out of these dresses. Or I would get some off the market. When [the children] were tiny, I bought it off the market and then I would do smocking and make all these pretty smocking dresses. I used to do them by hand before I got a machine.

There was also a knife grinder who called every now and then to sharpen knives, scissors and shears. He used to come until the late 1970s. And there was a van which came round selling bottles of lemonade and other fizzy pop drinks.

The first shop to appear in Sopwell, apart from those in Old London Road, was in Prospect Road. This used to be a post office until 2009. It was built when the new part of Prospect Road and St Julians Road were built in the 1920s and it sold everything, including clothes. In the Mandeville School Coronation Show brochure, there was an advertisement for A & L Martin, family grocers at 70 Prospect Road. They sold sausages, Saxby's pies and other cooked meats. Some time in the 1970s, an ex-sailor in the Merchant Navy bought the shop and had it converted into a post office. Two other owners followed and it was then closed for a couple of years, 1981–2. The present owner says that he bought it in 1983. It was originally much larger, but is now half the size, the other half being his sitting-room.

The Vesta Avenue parade of shops came next in the 1930s, and the ones in Cottonmill Lane were built just before the war as part of the Mentmore estate. The parade of shops in Abbots Avenue West was the last to be built before we had Sainsbury's and the Griffiths Way Retail Park in the 1990s.

Originally, there were four shops in Cottonmill Lane. Today, there is just one, Weymans (previously Archers). Weymans used to be two shops. On the opposite corner were another two. Margaret Brown remembers that, during the war, one was used as an ARP place. Two of them were let early: a sweet-shop/newsagents and a general grocer but the other two remained empty for some time because of the uncertainty of the war. Over the years the shops have been occupied by a butcher, a fishmonger, a grocer, a greengrocer and a newsagent. Two of them were converted into private apartments, and the other two joined together to become just one general store. In 1953, Vic Foster was employed as a paperboy with Mr Falke who ran the newsagent's on the corner of Mentmore and Cottonmill where the flats are now. He can remember the butcher's shop, Doffs stores (grocer's) on the other side and next to Falkes was a greengrocer and later a wet fish shop.

In the early years of the estates, money was tight and residents used to have food and other items on credit. Lil Day remembers getting her groceries from Doffs this way:

> He was a smashing bloke, Mr Bird. We used to down on a Friday and pay the bill and then on Saturday we would put it on the book again. Regular. Most of the people did. That's the way it was done.

On the corner of Leyland Avenue near where the youth club building is, there was a shoe repairer who was deaf and dumb. Lil Day remembers that he had an old concrete shed in which he used to do all his shoe repairing. Pamela Marshall said that, although he was deaf, he always understood exactly what was wanted and always did a superb job at a very reasonable price.

In Vesta Avenue there was a greater variety of shops than we have today. When they were first built, there were only three units: the two end shops and the butcher's, run by R.E. Holdham, in the middle. The middle shop was intended to be an off-licence run by Watney's brewery but this did not happen. The off licence went to the first shop, Grout's.

The other shops were built between them much later.

Vic Foster took over the butcher's in 1972. Before that he was employed as a manager with Holdham's. Holdham's was double fronted. When Vic first moved into the shop, he traded from the left-hand side. They used the whole of the shop but the counter was on the left and the refrigerated units were on the right. His landlord, Tony Holdham, the son of R.E. Holdham, lived in the flat above.

Vic Foster
1990s
Courtesy
Vic Foster

Vic Foster:

When I bought the business in 1972, I said I don't want this whacking big shop so I cut it in half. Peter Holdham had it altered to make a small shop on the left-hand side, so I moved into the right-hand side. The first lot to move into the shop next door were Howard's the baker's. Next door to Howard's baker's, when I moved in, was Ted and Hilda's hardware shop. Their surname was Ewer. Next door to them was Flora Fruits which was a greengrocer's and they sold flowers as well. They used to have an open front, no glass. They used to push up the shutters. That was owned by someone called England. Then there was a wool shop run by Franklin. The fish shop was the other side of my shop. It was a big shop and that was sort of cut in half and they had freezer sales on the left, not freezer goods, although they might have done. And the fish shop on the right also became a wet fish shop for a time . . .

Before the fish and chip shop, there was the cobbler's: Tom the cobbler. He always used to have second-hand shoes in the window belonging to the people who failed to collect them. The left-hand side of his shop was blacked out because he had his workshop there. It was all very dingy and full of dust. You also had Granville Supplies. Going back to the other side [Tavistock end], the first shop was Grouts. They had a grocery store with an off-licence in there and his wife used to have a hairdresser's upstairs. Then going back the other way, you had Woods the chemist. Mr and Mrs Mansell worked in there before Woods and then came Stephen Wise. The very end shop was the post office in the paper shop.

Barnaby Norman remembers the fish and chip shop when they gave away the fish and chips and charged for the salt and vinegar. That was the time VAT was put on fish and chips. In those days, the shops closed from 1–2pm for lunch and at midday on Thursdays.

By 1991, there were two general stores, one had a post-office and the other had an off-licence. The post-office had old wooden shelving. They later shared their premises with Woods the chemist until the proprietors retired to Mersea Island. Now it is part of Londis.

Cheong's, the fish shop and Chinese takeaway, is considered by many to be the best fish and chip shop in St Albans.

After over forty years of trading, Vic Foster retired in October 2006. Chris Pudsey describes Vic Foster as 'a proper old-fashioned shopkeeper'. Having grown up in Cottonmill, Vic knew everyone. His shop was the main centre of gossip in the area, and there was no question of popping in quickly for a few slices of ham. People say that he used to look out for his older customers, and if they didn't turn up when expected, he would investigate. He supplied meat on very good terms to St Stephen's lunch club and for church socials. He had many loyal customers and his business managed to survive several setbacks including the advent of Sainsbury's and a fire in 1988 when thousands of pounds'-worth of meat was ruined. This was caused by a faulty refrigerator unit and the shop had to close for three months. He and his wife, Vera, now drive the minibus which collects people for the St Stephen's lunch club, so they have been able to keep in touch with many of their previous customers.

The baker's was very popular especially with the builders working locally. They sold excellent jam doughnuts. However, the business declined towards the end and had to close. The two shops were joined together again and became a Caribbean restaurant for a brief time. It is now an Indian takeaway.

The Abbots Avenue West shops were in the planning stage in 1952. A report in the *Herts Advertiser* said drawings were being prepared for six shops and twelve flats. They probably opened in about 1953. Alfie Francis remembers when there was a butcher's shop, wool shop, a Co-op, a greengrocer and a newsagent in Abbots Avenue West. In the 1960s, Irene Ewer remembers that there was a hardware store (later an aquarium shop), a wool shop which was run by Mrs Saunders, a butcher's, a sweetshop/newsagent (now the hairdresser's), the Co-op (now Spar), and another sweetshop which is now Costcutter. There used to be a cigarette machine and a bubblegum machine outside the Co-op.

Before the King Offa pub was built, Pamela Marshall recalls that the area was just wasteland.

> We used to dig holes in it and make a little camp. It was scrubland from where the pub is to the railway for a long time.

Later streets

Prior to 1976, the land where Old Sopwell Gardens is now was used for allotments and was designated a public open space. Some time in 1976, the council decided to develop part of this land. This was unusual as the land was on the green belt. However, as there were no neighbours to object the freehold was sold to a developer. When the detailed plans were drawn up, objections came in from Prospect Road and St Julians Road resident groups. These were ignored and the building went ahead. The council said that this development would complement the proposed garage redevelopment adjacent to the Cottonmill allotments on the opposite side of the road. This development eventually became Nunnery Stables, and was built on the land where the riding stables once were but which had been replaced at some time later by garages.

Mercers Row, off Wilshere Avenue was built in the early 1980s.

The land on which many of the developments off Holyrood Crescent were built was sold by the Earl of Verulam in 1952 to Herts County Council. This land would have originally been part of Little Sopwell Farm. Kempe Close, Howland Garth and Coningsby Bank were built in the late 1950s. Ashdales was built in 1985. Watling View School sold part of their grounds for housing and Ashby Gardens was built on this land.

Just beyond Ashdales on Holyrood Crescent is Remus Close. This is built on the site of what was once Mandeville Children's Home which had been there since the late '60s. The home was knocked down in 2001 to make room for a small group of town houses. Chris Pudsey watched the demolition process from her garden.

In 1992, a developer was given the go-ahead to complete the 18-house estate on Old Oak which was in the green belt. There were already seven houses facing Cottonmill Lane and eleven more were to be built. That was when the access road was cut through the estate to reach the original Marlborough Club.

Demolition of Mandeville children's home 2001
© Chris Pudsey

Cottonmill Lane and beyond from the golf course
© Sandy Norman

The original London Road crossing the golf course 1970s Courtesy Peter Wares

Butcher with horse and cart Courtesy Vic Foster

Above: Flooded path through Fenny's Wood 2007
© Sheila Artiss

Below: Fenny's Boardwalk 2011
© Sandy Norman

View of the river and old watercress beds from the golf course
© Andy Webb

Chapter Seven
Sopwell at play

This chapter describes the recreational activities available in Sopwell and what residents did to amuse themselves. It is also about the green spaces and the river and how lovely and wild it must all have been before the pre- and post-war developments took place.

Children living in Sopwell before the estates were completed were lucky to have so many areas to explore. In those days they were free to wander everywhere without too much parental control. There were fields, woods and the river to play in and the roads were fairly free of cars so there was little danger of being run over. There were also many pockets of unused or undeveloped land on which to play. John Buckingham and his friends had great fun building dugouts and bonfires, as well as playing cricket and football, on the unused land between the Hatfield railway line and Leyland Avenue. Mrs Terry remembers that the boys played cricket in the field behind the Vesta Avenue shops because it was a good place for playing. Kathy Sinfield remembers playing cricket in the field where Praetorian Court is now. She said that there were so many fields before the houses were built that the children could play anywhere.

Bill Mackenzie was a bit of a lad and was always getting into mischief. He had many interesting tales to tell of his childhood exploits. Here are some of them:

When I lived in Cottonmill Crescent, Mum would give me sixpence. The choice was to buy a big bottle of Tizer or get the train to Park Street. We used to go to Park Street recreation ground. They used to have a massive big brass slide. It's got to be 20 feet high – there was nothing like it in St Albans. How Park Street got it I don't know! We felt it was worth our while to go over there. We tossed up between getting a bottle of pop or getting the train or we'd get a bottle of lemonade and we would walk to Park Street. We used to walk along the railway line, we weren't supposed to but we did. You used to get loads of wild strawberries along there in the season and there were cherry trees and pear trees along there. Up here on the Orbital you got a little cattle bridge from Hedges Farm. There used to be a big pear tree growing up there and you could stand on a bit of the bridge and pick the pears off the tree. They were little ones and hard as nails but we used to think it was great! We used to eat those old crab apples. Then you'd sneak along and come out by Park Street station. There was a path straight down the railway line which used to bring me out into the lane, Park Street Lane, and straight into the recreational ground . . .

I was still living in Cottonmill Crescent when they put a new sewer in and it went right the way across the golf course. We got into it on one of the tees. There was a brick building and you went in there. This was on a Sunday when there was nobody about. We climbed down this drainpipe and we got nearly all the way to Longmire Road. Then we thought we had better get out now while we can. There was no sewage going to come down as it hadn't been connected. We must have gone at least half a mile or three-quarters of a mile underground . . .

There used to be a sewer pipe down by the Nunnery on the river Ver about 300 yards on the Longmire Road side. There was a big outlet and it comes out to Old London Road and into Paxton Road. Often we used to go over there . . . and pick bits and pieces off the allotments, nick a few tomatoes and go and sit because where it came out to the river there was a nice brick pier and you could sit there and eat your tomatoes and bits and pieces that you had nicked off the allotments . . .

We used to go down where the entrance is to the allotments by the old swimming pool. There was a big air raid shelter there. That was our playground as well. It used to be black as ink when you got in. All the old iron strapped bunks were still in there. I remember going in there and cutting these strips of metal off and we used to put them on planks and make a sledge with a nice steel runner. It was about 1947 and I was only little and the snow was up to here [waist high]. We were over the golf course and we used to take our sleds. We used to go right the way down Cottonmill Lane on a sledge – there was still traffic there but we could have a go at it . . .

As I was saying, we used to walk across the road down the field. There was a little footpath there – that was before the M10 – and then we used to go straight up to the wood which was in Chiswell Green (Greenwood Park) and we used to go up there blackberrying. There were a lot of blackberries around, you could get a couple of baskets full then. And we used to go up further, go up King Harry Lane before you get to Waitrose by that St Albans School playing fields, the footpath goes up there. There was a big wood that the M10 went through – right through the middle. We used to go up there when it was legal to go and pick bluebells for your mum. It was beautiful up there, everywhere you went you were actually treading on a bluebell. There were thousands of them up there.

Lil Day said that her son, Keith, told her that there was a man called Sid who worked at Pearce's scrap yard in Cottonmill Lane. He would stand out in the front of the yard and children on their way to school at St Peter's would shout, 'Hey Sid have you got any ball bearings for us?' Sid gave some to the kids and they used them in their marble games. One young boy never wore pants under his trousers and the others would ask him to carry these ball bearings in his pockets knowing full well that by the time he reached school his trousers, weighted down by the ball bearings, would have fallen down.

Green spaces

Fortunately, despite all the estate development, there are still plenty of green spaces in Sopwell for leisure activities such as picnics, kicking a ball around or just a taking a stroll.

St Stephen's field between Watling Street and Praetorian Court in Wilshere Avenue is a beautiful green space with some of our most ancient trees. One of the oldest is the cedar which is estimated to be over five hundred years old. Legend says that Henry VIII courted Anne Boleyn underneath it.

Sopwell Nunnery green space in Cottonmill Lane, where the ruins are, has had Green Flag status for the past few years. It is a well managed and beautiful place now but it was quite wild and marshy at one time. Until the late 1960s, the area in front of the ruins was full of scrap metal and waste materials and children used this area as a playground. The wooded area by the river was also a popular place for children to play.

The green space at the back of Cottonmill Lane at Old Oak, called the Marlborough playing fields, has lovely views across the Ver valley and the golf course. The site is now being used as a multi-use games area. The grass is also laid out for football and there are changing facilities in the Marlborough Pavilion.

The green walkway by the Ver river between Cottonmill Lane and Holywell Hill, called Pocket Park, and the grassy area on Holyrood Crescent bordering the farmland are also lovely places to enjoy.

Verulam Golf Club

Sopwell's largest green space is Verulam golf course which is on our east border; from here there are magnificent views of the Ver valley. The golf course was once part of Sopwell Park. The original medieval road from London, a public right of way, runs right across the golf course. This same stretch of land was used for the St Albans Steeplechase in the 1800s.

The golf course is set in 60 hectares of gently undulating, free draining parkland. Bounded by the main railway line, Cottonmill Lane, London Road and the river, it is a good area to spot wildlife. In the Verulam Golf Club Centenary brochure, the course is aptly described as 'an oasis in the city'.

In the late nineteenth century, some local entrepreneurs approached Lord Verulam to grant an initial five-year tenancy to release the land to build the golf course. The tenancy was granted and the course, originally a nine hole layout set in 70 acres of arable land between Cottonmill Lane and Hedges Farm, was landscaped in the early 1900s. It opened in 1905. At the end of the five years, a further lease of twenty-one years was agreed and permission was granted to extend the layout to eighteen holes. This was opened in 1912. The freehold of the land was eventually purchased by the club in 1982. Samuel Ryder was the first captain. It was he who gave the Ryder Cup to the nation in 1927. Another famous member was Abe Mitchell who was Sam Ryder's personal coach. Abe was regarded by many as Britain's finest professional player at the time although he never won an Open Golf tournament The figure depicted on the lid of the Ryder Cup is Abe Mitchell.

In the First World War, some of the course was dug up to grow crops for the war effort.[130] During the Second World War, the club managed to avoid having to use the land for agricultural purposes by agreeing to allow sheep to be evacuated from Romney Marshes onto the golf course. This was supposedly to prevent the Germans eating the livestock if they invaded via the marshes. The sheep were accepted by the golfers who continued to play while they were there. The sheep also helped the mowing of the grass. There is an amusing tale about one of the players who managed to hit the ball into the flock which somehow landed in 'the posterior orifice' of one of the sheep. The unfortunate animal galloped off at a fast rate to the tenth green where the ball promptly fell out.[131] However, it is not known whether it actually landed in the tenth hole.

Betty Terry, who lived next to the golf course in Sopwell Lodge in the 1930s, remembers playing on the golf course when she was a child. She and her brother walked across it on their way to Alma Road School. She remembers Abe Mitchell and of course Samuel Ryder:

> They used to hit the ball over the road and over this great big pit. I remember that pit because when we came home from school I used to run past it in case there was anybody in there . . . When we lived at the Lodge, they had these golfing tournaments, and very often when the golfers came by on a hot day they wanted water, so we used to give them some water and one

of them suggested why don't we open a little shop and sell lemonade and everything but we wouldn't have been allowed to do it in those days because the farmer or Major Barnett [who lived in New Barnes House] would have stepped in and said you can't do that.

However, later residents of Sopwell Gate Lodge were much more enterprising and did sell refreshments to the golfers.

Children had a roaring trade in retrieving lost golf balls. Mr Golding, a resident of Longmire (Riverside) Road writing before the Second World War, recalls that he had a pole with a wire net on the end to retrieve golf balls from the river to sell to Abe Mitchell. [132]

Bill Mackenzie:

I often walked from where the golf course starts at the back of Sopwell [Home] Farm and walked down the river because you could feel all the golf balls under your feet. I used to pick them up and take them to the clubhouse and you would sell them to the pro up there for practice balls.

Nowadays, there are strict rules against trespassing. Only members and permitted visitors are allowed to access the course. The area is outstandingly beautiful with many ancient trees, and the area by the river and the disused watercress beds, now undisturbed by man, is truly wild.

Apart from all the famous golfers who have played at the club, one other famous visitor was Billy Graham, the evangelist, who played at the club in 1957.

Aerial view of the golf course with London Road station and Priory Park 1927 © English Heritage. NMR Aerofilms Collection

Cottonmill swimming baths

River Ver near Cottonmill Lane swimming baths *c.* 1970s Courtesy Betty Cutler

The open-air swimming baths in Cottonmill Lane were opened in 1905. However, some form of bathing facility in the river was there long before they were built. An article from the *Herts Advertiser* of 1st June 1861 says:

> We are glad to find the young men of St Albans are making an effort to secure a suitable bathing place, in the river Ver, near the site of the late Cotton Mill, where it is proposed to put up a bathing house, and to adapt the river to the intended purpose. If carried out this will tend to promote health and cleanliness; and we hope the regulations and terms will be so liberal as altogether to obviate the possibility of being reproached with having 'unwashed artisans' amongst us.

Despite this early promise of public swimming baths, they were not established on the site until 1883. Although the word 'Baths' appears on the 1898 OS map, this was not a proper bathing house as the baths were part of the river. An area of about 120 feet, which had a suitable depth for swimming, described as being between the Cottonmill bridge and Holywell meadow, was enclosed and the banks of the river were lined with wooden planks, including the ends.[133] The channel was deepened a little to give a depth of three to five feet. The bathers, probably just men, changed on the riverbank and a hut was constructed to give them some privacy. Diving took place from a concrete platform. The swimming and diving area could not have been very safe or clean, though, as this extract of 1890 notes:

> Swimming baths. Anyone who visits the present institution in Cotton Mill-lane [*sic*], dignified with the title of St Albans Swimming Baths will know what a dreadful travesty they are. A beginner who has to touch the bottom to learn is in fear that every moment his feet may be cut by a sharp flint stone, or else in the next minute he may be up to his knees in mud. The accommodation for diving is wretched, and the wooden planks which line the sides are covered with slime and are most unpleasant.[134]

This bathing facility probably did not last very long as the lack of a decent, clean place to swim led to a public campaign, led by Alderman George Slade, to rectify the matter. The baths, which are still there today, were opened on 29th July 1905. Alderman Slade, unfortunately, did not live to see them. The leader column in the *Herts Advertiser* of 5th

August 1905 said:

> For years the need of swimming and other baths has been keenly felt and successive Mayors, stimulated by the earnest appeals of the late Alderman Slade, exercised that influence which they possessed to supply a need which was felt and clamoured for.

The mayor, Horace Slade, the son of the late Alderman Slade (and local straw hat manufacturer) proudly gave an address at the opening ceremony. The article in the same edition of the *Herts Advertiser* gives a very detailed account of the campaign for a public baths, the ceremony and details of the construction and size of the pool, how much it cost and so on (see Appendix 3).

Despite the fact that the baths were very popular, there were still those who felt they had to complain. In 1932, a letter complaining about the accommodation was published in the *Herts Advertiser*:

> On a recent Sunday morning there was a queue awaiting admission to the swimming baths reaching from the entrance to Cotton Mill-Lane showing that the accommodation although adequate 25 years ago is quite unfit to cope with the population of today. If the difficulties that we are told have been experienced in the provision of an up to date swimming bath cannot be overcome for a long period, what is to prevent a small portion of the lake at Verulamium being transferred into a St Albans Lido. Surely this could be arranged at a small cost to the rates?[135]

Betty Cutler remembers the swimming baths in the 1930s:

> I will always remember the river and the swimming baths. Mr and Mrs Cheeser used to be the caretakers of the baths, because they lived in a house next to the baths – on the corner of Cottonmill Crescent. You went in the baths, it was threepence or sixpence and you went and got undressed in the cubicles and you had a bag and you had to take it back to Mr Cheeser or Mrs Cheeser and she used to give you a ticket. My brother used to use the baths a lot, I didn't. He was always down there, he was like a little fish. He used to help Mr Cheeser to sweep up. There was a turnstile to get in.

St Albans Sub-Aqua Club pool in the old Cottonmill Swimming Baths 2007 © Sandy Norman

Pamela Marshall remembers the swimming baths in the 1940s and '50s:

Going to Sunday school in Lattimore Road on Sunday afternoons was lovely in the summer. We would walk past huge queues of people waiting to get into the swimming baths with their rolled up towels under their arms. On the way home we would hang on the bars watching the people inside having a wonderful time. Our family were friends with a family in Cottonmill Crescent. Their back garden backed onto the swimming baths. There was huge green metal fence towering up at the end of their garden and you could hear all the screams and laughter going on the other side.

John Buckingham hated the pool because the water was so cold:

. . . and that was a place of many, many hours and years of pain – almost breaking the ice at times to get in there and being blue and standing on the side and having swimming lessons. I never became a good swimmer but I am sure that if the water had been warmer, I might have done a bit better.

Betty Terry's children belonged to the Cottonmill Swimming Club:

It was never heated. It was quite a communal thing in those days because they used to go down there and the staff were very good and if it was too wet to swim they used to teach them chess. My daughter was quite clever at diving and we joined the Watford Swimming Club and they wanted her to carry on and train to be an Olympic swimmer but my husband said no. He said sports were for pleasure. He had ideals like my dad and said that nobody should be paid for sport. It should be a relaxation thing.

Jennifer Taylor remembers that the seats in the changing rooms were very rough so much so that:

you used to get splinters in your bottom!

Swimming galas were held in the pool every summer and schools sent the children there to swim. Unfortunately as it was not heated and open to the elements, it could only used for about three months of the year. In 1979, the County Education department decided to stop swimming lessons in the Cottonmill pool. The use of the pool had diminished and it was said to be wasting money. Then, with the opening of the Westminster Lodge leisure centre, the baths were eventually closed. The premises are currently used by the St Albans Sub-Aqua Club, familiarly known as 'the dive club'.

There was another swimming pool adjacent to the British Cardboard Box machine factory in Belmont Hill where Albeny Gate and de Tany Court are now. It was used by St Albans School. Vic Foster remembers skinny-dipping there in his youth.

The river

Today the river Ver can be described as just a pretty, fast-flowing chalk stream but not so long ago, before the water companies started to extract the water, it was a proper river and people used it for recreational purposes. The Ver has been canalised since Roman times so that now it flows in more or less straight lines. The river at the bottom of Holywell Hill, for instance, was diverted by the Spencer family for their water gardens. Such diversions are, of course, not natural and sometimes the river breaks free and floods the surrounding land. This is normal river behaviour and provides a home for a variety of wildlife in the surrounding water meadows. The river, and the springs which fed it, were essential to the watercress industry.

The Ver Valley Society was formed in November 1976 with the objective of improving all aspects of the river Ver, its valleys and its environs so to create a leisure and educational facility for the whole community.[136] There was great concern over the abstraction of water from the river by pumping stations further up the river by Redbourn. This was coupled with the drought of 1976 where the river almost dried up. Yet in the following two years there was an excess of rain with much flooding, especially on the allotments in Cottonmill Lane.

In 1987, writing about the state of the river, Miss Blower of Sopwell Mill Farm said that there had been a considerable decrease in the water flow since the water abstraction started with the result that the condition of the river water was so bad that her horses and cattle refused to drink from it. Each time it rained, oily water was disgorged from surface drain outlets so that the river was covered by a foul-smelling oily slick. She also said that before 1960, it was not possible to walk (in Wellingtons) along the bed of the whole stretch of the river on the farm (approximately half a mile); and that, at the ford by the house the water, in 1945, came almost to a horse's knees. In the 1920s the water level by the mill wheel was recorded as being four to five feet deep.[137]

Working with St Albans District Council, a scheme was devised in the mid 1970s to create a riverside walk. This was the Ver Valley walkway project which goes from St Michaels village to Moor Mill in Frogmore. As much of the river passes through Sopwell, the plan was to improve the area around the river, especially the open space by the ruins and the disused railway line to Hatfield, which eventually became the Alban Way. The initial plan was to open up the walkway from Holywell Hill behind Prospect Road through to Cottonmill Lane by the swimming baths, and this was eventually achieved, although not without a battle. Some Prospect Road residents fought the scheme as they said that their back gardens were an easy target for vandals. A petition signed by 54 residents said that vandalism was rife. One lady reported that youths threw a brick at her.[138]

The path from Cottonmill Lane as far as Sopwell Mill Farm was in existence at the time but was very overgrown. It is now well managed although there is no access to the farm from the path. In 2010, the Sopwell Residents Association applied for and obtained a Community Spaces grant from the Lottery funded Groundwork UK to build an all weather boardwalk and crushed concrete path. The walkway, now greatly improved, has been named Fenny's Boardwalk after the man who looked after the stables in Cottonmill Lane.

The next stretch, from Sopwell Mill Farm to New Barnes, is privately owned by the Gorhambury Estate, so permission would have to be obtained from the Earl of Verulam to use it. Members of the Verulam Golf Club are fortunate to able to see the river from their side as well as the lakes which were once watercress beds. Sea oyster shells have been found by the present tenants of Sopwell Mill Farm in a field in this stretch of the river. These may have been discarded as far back as the Roman occupation, confirming that the Ver was once a navigable river.

There used to be plenty of fish in the river. In the *Herts Advertiser* of 20th January 1978, there is a picture of a boy holding a trout fished from the river. John Buckingham and his mates fished for crayfish and at one time caught more than they bargained for:

> Down by river at the bottom of Holywell Hill we used to go in there catching crayfish – proper crayfish not the American ones. We used to take our buckets and our nets down there. We used to put them in the buckets. We were only catching them we weren't cruel to them. Once you caught so many you would let them out and just watch them swim off as fast as they could go. And one day we were down there we found a belt of ammunition with great big cartridges and as far as we know they were live . . . [they were] big shells between four and six inches long . . . where they come from we don't know . . . On the other side of the river to the waterworks, the Jet garage side, there was a factory and I think somebody told me they used to do ammunition during the war so whether that tied in I'm not sure . . . We took them up to the police station.

Children often paddled and swam in the millpond by New Barnes Mill. The water formed a natural pool about five foot deep – it was too deep to stand in mid-stream. The water was described as clear and sweet with a fine gravel bottom.[139] Kathy Sinfield's mother used to take eight or nine kids from the street down there to swim in the deeper part. Margaret Brown remembers that her playmates sometimes went round the back of the mill to where the water went into the wheel. She was very frightened of the deep water, and wouldn't go. Her mother had told her about how, when she herself was little, they played in the river by the Silk Mill, and a child had drowned there and been washed up at the bottom of Holywell Hill.

Bathing in the Ver near new Barnes in the 1930s
© Betty Terry

John Buckingham recalls happy times down by the river:

[We went into] what we used to call Browny's field. This is along from the corn mill. We used to go down the bottom of Cottonmill Lane, go straight across the field of the little first river which is the overflow bypass... go across a wooden bridge which would come out right behind where Sopwell House is now, where the hotel rooms are I believe. They used to be cowsheds and they used to have all numbers on and the cows looking out over their stalls. Then we'd follow the river along towards Park Street and you got to halfway along towards the North Orbital and it's where the junction of the bypass river, overflow river, the mill and the main river comes through and it is shallow there and we used to paddle and take our picnics there. We always loved these sunny days...

Kathy Sinfield and Joan Forder remember the bridges by New Barnes Mill:

And the little bridge when you got into the field, you could sit on it. My feet didn't reach there but of course the boys feet reached the river floor...

... it wasn't comfortable as well because it was iron and it had stones and that in it. The second one was, because it was a wooden bridge. We used to go across the wooden bridge and over a stile and you were in the farmer's field then and they used to tell you off sometimes.

Many residents called that part of the river, which flows past New Barnes, the Tar. William Goodman, born 1900, wrote in a letter to the Ver Valley Society in 1987:

Beyond New Barnes Mill as far as the A405, the river was known as the Tar river for reasons unknown.

In another letter to the Ver Valley Society, Mr G. Hall wrote:

Towards the end of the 1920s, we bathed and swam in a stretch of the river called the Tar river. This was nearer the village of Park Street where boating could be seen from the railway.

Kathy Sinfield and Joan Forder also called it the Tar. Kathy's parents also called it the Tar river so the name must go back several generations.

> Of course it was all fields round the back of us and right down through Cottonmill and up to about the borders of the golf course, Verulam golf course and then way down in the other direction going south to the orbital and the river there – it's called the river Ver but to us it was the Tar river – it was the Tar river and we used to take our jam jars and go tiddling . . . it was very clear, I remember, the water.

Margaret Brown thought that it was only the mill-race which was called the Tar. No-one seems to know why it had that name. Contrary to Kathy and Joan, Margaret Brown said it was always a bit grubby.

The river was a great boon to the area and locals used it for swimming, boating and fishing and in winter, if it was cold enough, for skating. In the Christmas holidays in the winter of 1890/91, it was reported that the 'ice was crowded at Sopwell . . . '[140] This was presumably near Sopwell House. Also between Sopwell ruins and the river, the ground was often flooded in winter and the children used to slide and skate on it.[141]

Mr Golding, a resident of Longmire (Riverside) Road, writing before the Second World War, recounts his memories of when he was a lad:

> Down near the bridge in Cottonmill Lane, the river was not all that deep – we used to paddle in it – but as you went farther along the river towards the golf course it got deeper in places. Where the flats are in Riverside Road [there were] allotments and one day there was a big storm and the river burst its banks and flooded the allotments . . . when they dried up there were one or two small pikes left on the ground dead.[142]

He goes on to say that there were watercress beds on either side of the Great Northern Railway bridge and that the water under the bridge was not all that deep. It became very muddy going towards the old mill, presumably New Barnes, where the Cottonmill Club was. There were more watercress beds across the river from the golf course end roughly from the sixth tee to the seventh fairway. (Any golfers reading this will know that the layout of the Verulam golf course changed and so the tees and greens described here are different from what they are now.)

> The river at the fifth green varies from deep to muddy. About 100 yards from the green going down river you could swim in parts of it . . . you had to go past the seventh tee to swim in places . . . we were not allowed but we went in the river. Going along towards the old Co-op [New Barnes] Mill were some willow trees and we used to call it Jack's Island and you could swim there – that was about 200 yards from the mill. Past the mill going towards the arterial road [North Orbital], the river did not seem all that deep . . . There was plenty of bird life and rats.[143]

Mrs Murray of Longmire Road writing from 1937 onwards said:

> Our backyard came down to Pinnock's watercress beds. We had an allotment by the river and every time we had a storm, the river overflowed and our vegetables were under water for about a week. There was a heron – they also got in the watercress beds. The river was full of tiddlers, sticklebacks etc. and in the spring we had hundreds of tiny frogs and at night they would sit around the street lamp and eat flies and moths attracted by the light. The river that ran through the golf course was very deep and a child drowned in it. The big boys used to dive off a willow tree and swim.[144]

John Buckingham and his friends once had a 'seaworthy' boat:

> The older boys had a boat, a second-hand boat from the Sea Cadets down the Verulamium lake. It was pretty old and ropey and could just about float and they were given permission to collect it. They went down and they floated it . . . and pushed it under the bridges. It was too shallow, the Ver, under the bridges but it floated in other places and they took it right the way down to what I call our woods, the woods behind Sopwell Nunnery . . . It was something we

always wanted. We used to try and float anything, rafts, baths, old tin baths but they had too many holes in. It was like sitting in a watering can! . . . Well the bigger boys got this boat . . . and my Dad and a couple of the fathers got some pitch from the gasworks and . . . they made it watertight. Where we used to keep it was in an inlet in the woods [near the boardwalk] that was flooded Even in the summer it was boggy . . . We used to hide the boat in there . . . And on high days and holidays the bigger boys would push the boat out in the main stream [between Cottonmill and the railway bridge]. You could float the boat quite easily. As usual, a gang, I don't know who it was, somebody discovered it and took it out from our hiding place and then let it out on the river and it went down to the railway bridge and it must have beached there.

Years later, John happened to meet someone who worked for the river board who told him they found this boat, towed it away and then smashed it up.

The area beyond New Barnes on the way to Park Street was a popular spot for courting couples to have picnics. Lil Day said that when she first came to St Albans, she lived with her mother-in-law in Park Street until her husband came out of the forces:

And the River Ver was at the bottom of the garden. Where we lived was right in the main part right opposite the Swan which has been pulled down, and next door to the Post Office. And we had the river down below and somebody had got a boat, a really old one, no oars. So there was me, my husband and his two brothers and their wives and we got a picnic with us and we had a wind-up gramophone and we got broomsticks and punted way up to Cottonmill. We went under bridge by the North Orbital and we got out and had our lunch on a grass patch – it was all grass then. And we had music. And then we went back and they put their poles in where it was too muddy and they ended up in the water!

Pamela Marshall said that:

In the summer holidays, a favourite pastime for my sisters and I was walking down to the little bridge by the [New Barnes] Mill, hitching our skirts up into our knickers and paddling in the river. We always took condensed milk and sugar sandwiches, a bottle of sherbet and water, a jam jar and our funny little nets. We would try to catch sticklebacks and tadpoles, it was such fun.

The watercourse was cleaned out regularly to keep it free of weeds and other debris. John Buckingham:

Once or twice a year the men would be in the river always cleaning it out and then they would have a boat in the river with like a paddle on it, a blade on it and they would go up and down cutting the reeds and lay a net down further and they'd go down with the flow of the water into the net and they would pull out all the off cuts on to the bank.

Lil Day's son Keith used to get up to mischief:

The chaps used to have a boat to keep the river Ver clean, cutting the weeds down and he said that when they came out of school, up St Peter's School there, we used to see these blokes cutting the edge. The boat was moored by the swimming baths there. He said they would look to see where the men were and would jump in the boat, him and his mates, and they would go all the way down to the bottom of Holywell Hill and leave the boat there. And then they would go along Prospect Road and home.

A member of the Ver Valley Society and an artesian well sinker by profession, Mr Edward Butcher kept a log of river activities in 1978 and 1979. Eddy Butcher was Betty Cutler's father. In the hot summer of 1976, many will remember the river almost drying up, whereas in 1978 and 1979, it flooded the allotments:

We have had a lot of rain in July [1978] but in the first week of August we have had thundering rain and it has come down in as you can say cloudbursts. Now I have only known in my lifetime the allotments flooding twice and each time it's been in the spring and not in August. The river is choked with weeds and with the torrential rains it has overflowed at the lowest place where the bank is shallow and the water is laying about a foot in the soil and it is going to take a long time before it goes down . . . there is at least eight foot of peat before it can soak into the gravel and get away. Also the torrential rains flooded the fields near Sopwell Farm but that cleared in ½ hour but as I have said before, the river cannot flow fast as the weeds stop the flow. Perhaps it's a good thing as there might be a lot of flooding down the low parts of the river. I'll just say why the allotments got flooded, [it] was the storm water rushing into the river at St Michael's, Holywell Hill, the town centre and Old London Road storm water pipes and being stopped with the reeds that are growing in the river. That is why the allotments got flooded at the lowest bank at the corner of the allotments . . .

. . . This is April 10th 1979, and as we are getting a lot of rain the river is still running fast and high. That is another point to remember as we have had more rain and snow since Christmas for more than 30 or 40 years. If we could get our normal seasons the river would still run nicely when the pumping stops. And also the allotments are flooded the same as last year . . . There used to be cress beds near the Prospect Road gardens and also a deep ditch but they have been filled in. Also the ditch ran into the river and you can see the course which the water went since this flooding started.

The water meadows at Sopwell provide a habitat for a variety of wildlife. Many different birds, moths, butterflies, frogs and toads have been recorded especially during the first half of the last century. There was a variety of wildflowers then, including red campion, ladies smock, cowslip, forget-me-not, yellow iris, bittercress, white meadow saxifrage, kingcups, ragged robin and toadflax, all growing by the river because it was so damp.[145] In the stretch of river which is inaccessible to the public, from Sopwell Mill Farm to New Barnes Mill, there is an abundance of wildlife. Egrets, freshwater mussels, crayfish, trout and chub have all been spotted.

Riverside Road Fisheries

The Verulam Angling Club was formed in 1934. The fishing lake in Riverside Road is only one of many sites in the district managed by the club. In the 1960s, work was started on the site in Riverside Road which was dug out of one of the disused watercress beds.

Verulam Angling Club fishing lake in Riverside Road
© Sandy Norman

Since then it has been extended and has become one of the prime local fishing lakes. It is situated in idyllic surroundings and is one of Sopwell's hidden gems. Unfortunately, access to the site is for members only but there is an open day for the public to view, once a year. The club controls a wide variety of coarse fishing as well as some close season fishing for trout and says it offers everything from big carp (up to over 40lb), barbel, bream and pike, to small river dace and chub. Much to the annoyance of the fishermen, the lake is also home to the invasive signal crayfish which have escaped from the river. These have to be cleared out annually. All their waters are maintained through regular working parties to ensure they offer safe and comfortable fishing, with nearly half of the club's annual income invested in improvements and restocking.[146]

The allotments

Sopwell had several areas of allotments especially before the post-war estates were built. In the mid 1920s, there were two areas of allotments: the Hare and Hounds allotments (the area below the inn) and the Cottonmill allotments on the other side of Cottonmill Lane. Opposite the swimming pool, the ground was not considered to be as good, as it was quite stony. That was the land on which the new St Peter's School was built.

People even cultivated the spaces between the Hatfield and Watford railway lines. John Buckingham's father rented a plot from the railway company during the 1940s and 50s.

> ... Every bit of land was dug up to grow vegetables, people don't remember. My dad rented a piece of ground near the big signal posts as you approach St Albans Abbey station, which was at the bottom of Leyland Avenue ... A short siding ran out from where the signal box was at the bottom of St Julians Road. The allotments were at the side by the buffers. Dad used to take us across there, crossing the lines ... the same way he used to go to work for most of his life, and we used to merrily dig away and I used to help him in my little way ... When you think, we were right next to a full-size railway in operation! ... At a later time, [I think] it was summertime because all the plants had been set. My dad was very proud of his garden. It was about ten pole or something like that, and it was all set and I came out the back coming from school or playing and mum said, look it's a bulldozer over on your dad's allotment down the bottom of the garden and I looked over and there was a big yellow bulldozer going over, up and down, flattening all my dad's plants which were well on the way to maturing and ready to pick. Mum yelled across to the man and he just looked the other way and carried on going backwards and forwards ... After quite a long battle, my father did receive compensation, I can't remember but it was something ridiculous like 7 shillings and sixpence for all his hard work and not really [receiving] an apology saying it was one of the clauses that if they wanted their land back or something then they could have it anytime ... They wanted to extend the railway line up to the cutting. What was annoying to us, it must have been, I guess, six or eight years, something like that, before they even did it; that's typical.

The cutting referred to by John was the one from the level crossing towards the King Offa pub. He remembers when it was dug out.

Today there are three rentable areas which are in Cottonmill Lane, by Sopwell Mill and in the Nunnery open space. Being adjacent to the river, these sites have always been prone to flooding as we have seen from Eddy Butcher's account above. John Buckingham remembers having to walk to St Peter's School in wellingtons down a flooded Cottonmill Lane during many winters and being amused to see old disused carts floating around in the allotments. His father rented another allotment where Old Sopwell Gardens is now:

> ... opposite used to be the gate to the allotments and that's where we had our allotments there under where the new houses are. I used to go down there with my dad. I used to love it down there and I would be sent off to the river to get water. The river was a lot deeper than it is now [but] there was never any need for fences or walls. You were quite a long way away and you were only small. You would go along with your buckets and dip in and get the water. They

didn't have water tanks and taps . . . and you'd bring it back and in a couple of minutes your dad would send you back down there again. It kept me out of mischief.

The allotments were often targets for anti-social behaviour. John said that quite often they would find that kids had ripped all their produce up.

Allotment holders have a thriving association to provide mutual help and advice: the Cottonmill and Nunnery Allotment Association, which was formed in 1994. The CNAA also holds social events including an annual summer show.

Nunnery 1 allotments 2011 © Sandy Norman

The Watercress Wildlife Association

When the watercress industry ceased in the 1970s, the area below Riverside Road was used partly for allotments and partly as builders' dumping ground. There was even a piggery there.[147] Eventually, the local residents decided to reclaim it and obtained permission to turn the area into a beautiful wildlife sanctuary. It was formally opened in 1991 and is home to many birds, butterflies, moths and bats. It also has a small apple orchard in the grounds. Anyone may visit and enjoy the area.

Sopwell Youth Club

The youth club behind Leyland Avenue was opened in 1970. It started up as a boys' club partly financed by county council grants. It has been a mixed blessing to the area. Not welcomed to start with, it was subject to much vandalism, and was neglected because of underfunding. Today, it is hardly used as the building can no longer be maintained.

The club was built on a plot of land that the children used as a general play area and somewhere to play football and cricket. John Buckingham, who lived in Leyland Avenue, said that the land was maintained and watched over by the local residents and was always kept clean. No-one dared drop even a sweet wrapper in case they incurred the wrath of 'elderly ladies'.

> A chunk of [our play area] was taken off because when they widened the lane here [Cottonmill] on the bridge, they doubled the width . . . 'Cos that used to be where we used to get our firewood for bonfires, a lot of it. Our camps used to be there . . . our dugouts which used to be along there, and that was a big play area. We made bike tracks on it, we did everything. And all of a sudden in the local papers . . . they were going to build a new boys' club adjacent to Cottonmill Lane so we all thought, where can that be, somewhere around the allotments down there? Anyway it turned out that it was on that piece of ground there. Well, the local people just didn't want it. They didn't want a boys' club built there, and what right had the council to take that piece of land because that [came] with the development of the houses? So there was a lot of bad will to start with. All of a sudden they came . . . and started digging the footings out and putting the footings in. Then I don't know how many times it happened, but a lot of the walls got pushed down, kicked down and it didn't go very well and they more or less had to put – not an armed guard on it – but they had to get it up quick. Anyway, it was built, and it was opened by one of the comedians, Derek Nimmo. I remember going to the opening . . . And I thought it was a good idea once it was there to make the most of it for the community and local boys and anybody to keep them out of mischief and so on – and they tried lots of different ways.

> I spent a lot of time there and what was heartbreaking was that you would spend hours working down there repairing something and then go next time and find that it was smashed . . . fire engine went down the side of the youth club and went straight in the drains because the covers weren't strong enough to take the fire engine, and I got some really heavy duty ones for them.

> It was used but it seems to have got run down more and more over the years. The boys' club was there for quite a few years. They might have had a spell when they had a mixed club there. We had a club that used to run down there, a badminton club. When we used to use it, we used to clean it and always leave it tidy. It was a happy little club at one time . . . you help out where you can but then you get so frustrated when you see something that's wrecked the day after you have done it, it gets heartbreaking. You re-hang a door and the next day it has been kicked off . . . A chap called Doug Dorling and myself and the committee, we tried to keep it running with the local authority. The funding was cut back, and it would go so long and then it would almost fold up . . . Now you go round there and it's disgusting. It's all falling to bits.

According to an article about vandalism at the club in the *Review* in 1976, 33 boys aged between eight and eleven met there regularly. The fire doors had had to be nailed up as the club was unable to afford to pay for essential repairs. One set of doors had been ripped from the hinges and dumped on the grass. Doug Dorling, who ran the club on a voluntary basis, said that the building had been badly designed which made the doors very vulnerable.[148]

There were other clubs for boys in Sopwell: the 4th St Albans Scouts and the Boys Brigade. The 4th St Albans Scouts, which is still going strong, meets in the Jim Green Memorial scout hut in Riverside Road. The Boys Brigade was active in the 1970s and 1980s. They had their meetings in St Julian's Church.

Cottonmill Club and the Marlborough playing fields

A social club, called the Cottonmill Club, was launched in the late 1960s to provide community facilities for the residents of the new Cottonmill and St Julian's estates. Membership was by subscription, and in its heyday it attracted over 2,000 members. The community centre was situated approximately where the car park to the Marlborough Pavilion is today in Old Oak, Cottonmill Lane, although Old Oak was not built until several years later. The club was a popular venue for dancing, especially among the elderly on the estate.[149]

Boys Brigade in
the 1970s
Courtesy Lee
Welch

St Albans Buggy Club 1987 © Vic Foster

Within the community centre, a group of pensioners ran their own club, called the Get Together Club. They organised coach trips and theatre visits, and had fundraising activities where they made and sold their own toys and clothes.[150] John Buckingham's mother and Betty Cutler's father, Edward Butcher, were members. John said the club decorated a float for the St Albans Carnival for many years.

By August 1986, membership of the main social club had dropped considerably and it was reported to be in financial difficulties. It was too expensive to maintain. In 1989 the club was facing bankruptcy with estimated debts of around £80,000–100,000. Membership was down to 700 residents.[151] The reason given for the falling numbers was that most of the original members were now elderly and no longer keen to participate. The demographic had changed from young families to an aging population.

The club was shut down in 1990, but reopened ten months later with a change of name. Now called the Marlborough Club, membership was again by subscription and it attracted 300 members. However, in 1994 the club was destroyed by fire and was not rebuilt because the insurance payout fell short of rebuilding costs. Instead, a more modest building called the Marlborough Pavilion was built as a meeting room and changing area for sports. Today, there are plans to extend the building to make it more of a community centre again.

In the grounds of the community centre, there was at one time a racing car club for model radio controlled cars run by Vic Foster. In 1986, the track was laid out and built, originally of turf and soil, and later with a more permanent surface. Called St Albans Buggy Club, it was opened in February 1987 by the mayor, Ron Wheeldon. The club met every Sunday morning and raced in three classes: expert, intermediate and junior leagues. To start with they had 25 members (boys only) aged between eleven and nineteen but at one time they had 60. The club had its own equipment shed. This was vandalised many times and eventually burnt down. The track can still be seen on the left side of the field down the slight slope, but it is very overgrown. Vic Foster also ran a darts team at the King Offa pub.

Hunting

During the nineteenth and early twentieth centuries, and maybe earlier, hunting with dogs took place in Sopwell even though there are no written reports of their activities or where the pack went. However, we can make educated guesses based on what people remember. We do know that in the mid nineteenth century, Silvester, who was the farmer at Hedges Farm, was granted the right to hunt on his land.

The hounds were kept in kennels in Fenny's stables in Cottonmill Lane where Nunnery Stables is now, and many remember the hunt going off on Sunday mornings through the fields towards Park Street. Old Mr Pinnock (who owned the watercress beds) was a hunt member.[152]

Betty Terry remembers seeing the hounds being exercised in Cottonmill Lane:

The hounds used to come every week. They had a St Albans hunt and they used to bring the hounds for exercise down the lane.

Vera Foster remembers seeing them in Cottonmill Lane stables. She said the hounds went up Albert Street when her Mum was a kid in the 1920s.

A young Gerry Dunham remembers the hunt and the sound of the horn on a Sunday morning:

On a Sunday morning they came out all dressed up lovely. His name was Fenny. I was about eight. They were ever so smart with the dogs. They met down where the stables were and that's where they started. They used to toddle off over the wasteland over the fields towards Park Street over farmland, Hedges Farm. I used to say hello to him. He was very nice.

The hounds exercising in Cottonmill Lane c.1930 © Betty Terry

Other amusements

Many residents remember the travelling funfairs which were held in the 1950s and 1960s in the field facing the houses down Butterfield Lane. John Buckingham remembers that there were old steam engines inside the roundabouts.

Pamela Marshall:

A visit to the fair in Butterfield Lane was fun, especially as we were all forbidden to go! Walking down Gorham Drive was so exciting as we could hear the music playing. There was a chairo-plane, helter-skelter, and dodgems of course – all the boys loved the dodgems – and these huge swings (gondolas) which you pulled with a rope, and hoop-la and all the little sideshows. We always stayed too long and ran home as fast as our little legs could carry us. I can't remember whether the fair came once or twice a year. It always seemed to be dark so it must have been autumn or winter time.

Nancy Broadbent:

The playing field used to be the funfair. They used to come every year. We used to play on the penny machines and [when I ran out] I said to my friend, 'Hold the machines I'll go and get another penny,' and I would run all the way up the alleyway and across the road, Holyrood Crescent, up the alleyway to the top of Creighton Avenue and go and get a penny.

Betty Cutler remembers the gypsies and tramps who came knocking at the door:

I remember a woman knocking on my door when I lived in Cottonmill Crescent and I was expecting [my daughter] Joy, she said you'll get what you want and I wanted a girl bad. And she said you won't have any more. I always remember that . . . Tramps used to knock on the door and one [person] used to give him apples and a bit of tea and milk and others used to give him water so he had a billy can full of water so he could make some tea.

John Buckingham has fond memories of bonfire nights:

Behind Leyland Avenue where the youth club is, we always had a big bonfire there. What you've got to remember was that the lane itself was a narrow lane with rough woods up either side and it always used to be a job to get enough material to burn because you always tried to get the biggest bonfire with an extension ladder to put your guy on the top and one of my first memories was up in the woods – the wood at the side of the road. I was up there with my big brother, unfortunately trimming a few branches, the hawthorns and that and there was this voice come down; 'Oi, you lads in there.' You can imagine who it was, Mr Plod! But that was fun. At the end of the school holidays in September you started thinking of bonfires . . . The biggest problem was the other local lads who used to come and try and steal it. We had competition, there was another bonfire along this side of the railway, beside the cutting, and another over where the swings are just over the bridge, and ones up Doggetts, but there was a limit how far kids would drag wood. Eventually you got enough materials together and the big bonfire was something you would look forward to. It always seemed to be very cold or wet. And the fire was lit – if you could stop the other gangs from coming and lighting it as once you put your paper under it – because you formed a tunnel underneath – you were very prone to the other gangs coming along and putting a match to it . . . So you would guard it and the fire would go for at least a couple of hours. Then you always put your potatoes in the ashes and stand around talking, very neighbourly. It was a lovely atmosphere. You had fireworks but you didn't have all these massive great big things they have now.

On the right-hand side of Little Sopwell Farm, down Holyrood Crescent, is a barn on the where there was 'swap shop'. Items were brought there to be swapped for something else. Vic Foster remembers taking in an old carriage clock and swapping it for a set of car ramps. The barn, which still exists, may once have been a pigsty.

Sopwell Youth Club © Sandy Norman

Appendix 1
Fire at Sopwell Nunnery Farm 1931

What follows is the report from the *Herts Advertiser* of 20th February 1931 of a fire at Sopwell Nunnery Farm and the simple-minded chap who eventually confessed to starting it. Albert Evans of 44 Watson's Walk was charged with:

> feloniously setting fire to a wheat stack at Kingsbury Farm on Jan 23rd and also feloniously setting fire to Sopwell Nunnery Farm on Jan 21st.

In 1931, the Sopwell Nunnery Farm was a mixed farm and described as being 'in a somewhat isolated spot'. The lease at the time was owned by Edgar Percy Pearce of Link House Cunningham Avenue. The farm building was described as consisting

> of one long stone building divided into two sections, one used for stabling and livestock and the other half for storage purposes. Attached to the building was a large corrugated iron shed 60ft long, 24ft high and 14ft wide which was used for storage of waste paper. On Jan 21st there was about 400 tons of waste paper stored there.

The fire lasted for four days. The contents of the shed were completely destroyed, and the whole of the building practically destroyed. The damage done amounted to approximately £1,500. Pearce said that the accused was not employed by him and had no right to be on the premises.

From the descriptions given by witnesses, one can build a picture of what the farm and yard and the surrounding area must have looked like. At the time, Prospect Road, originally a cul-de-sac, had recently been cut through from the St Julians Road end to Cottonmill Lane, hence the references to New Prospect Road.

Henry Walter Javeleau of 41 Sopwell Lane, who was employed by Mr Edgar Percy Pearce as a paper baler, gave evidence. He said that the shed was stacked with bales from floor to roof and that there were no divisions, no steps or ladders and no room for anyone to lie between the top of the stacks and the roof. He said he was the last to leave, and there was no sign of fire then.

Another witness was Alfred Willis of 24 Longmire Road, a stockman employed by Mr Pearce. He said that on 21st January he was sorting scrap metal in the cowshed. When the workmen left at 5pm, he secured the cowshed as well as the fowl-houses, and that everything was in order when he left about 5.15pm. He returned at 7pm to feed the horse and the dog which were in the cowshed but there was no sign of a fire and he did not see anyone else there. He said there were about thirty head of poultry in the sheds. At 9.05pm, because of what someone said when he was in Holywell Hill, he returned to the farm which was then on fire. The Fire Brigade had just arrived and was at work. The horse, the dog and the poultry had all been released when he got there.

The next witness was Albert Edward Simmons, a carpenter who lived at a house called Lympne, New Prospect Road. He said that, at about 8.45pm on Wednesday 21st January, while he was walking along Cottonmill Lane near the entrance to the farm, he saw what he thought to be a bonfire, and, after he passed the gate to the farm, he noticed a lad knocking at the door of a cottage at the corner of Prospect Road. The lad, who he did not recognise, went to Mr Simmons and said something. In consequence, Mr Simmons looked in the direction of Sopwell Nunnery Farm and saw flames coming through the roof of the farm buildings at the further end. Mr Simmons and the lad went towards Mardale, New Prospect Road, to use the telephone, and met PC Lee. Mr Simmons spoke to the constable and then went back to the farm to render assistance in releasing the stock.

Francis James Turvey of 7 Longmire Road said he was walking along Cottonmill Lane with a lady friend and, when they turned into Prospect Road, the accused, whom they knew, pointed to Sopwell Nunnery Farm and said, 'Look at the fire!' After he had said that, Mr Simmons, who was with the accused, directed him to a house in Prospect Road where there was a telephone. The accused (Evans) ran off in that direction. Turvey said that he saw Evans speak to PC Lee, and then he and his lady friend and other people went to release the livestock at the farm. He then said that, when he was walking along Cottonmill Lane at about 6.40pm on the following day (22nd January), he saw Evans standing on the bridge near the swimming bath. Evans said to him, 'How did you get on last night? I have been here all night.' Turvey's lady friend, Violet Balls aged fifteen, of Prospect Road corroborated his evidence.

Hubert Victor Thorpe, the Chief Engineer and Secretary of St Albans City Fire Brigade, said that, at 9.02pm on Wednesday 21st January he received an alarm from the City Police Station. He turned out with other officers and two pumps and went to Sopwell Nunnery Farm. The barn and a shed full of paper were on fire. The brigade were engaged at the scene of the fire for three and a half days. He examined the place and was of the opinion that the fire either started with the galvanised iron building or with a heap of paper on the south-west side of it.

Hubert Leslie Thorpe, a member of the St Albans City Fire Brigade, said that, at about 1.30am on Thursday 22nd January, he was engaged with the brigade at Sopwell Nunnery Farm.

PC L.W. Lee said that at about 9pm on Wednesday 21st January he was patrolling near Prospect Road in the direction of Cottonmill Lane. When he was about sixty yards from the corner of St Julians Road, he saw fire and smoke coming from a small shed at the further end of Sopwell Nunnery Farm.

The accused, Albert Evans, said he wanted to tell the truth about the fire at Pearce's yard.

> About 9.30 on Wednesday January 21st, I walked down Cotton Mill-lane across the allotments round a large shed in the allotments along the path to the ruins. I then climbed over the fence, had a look around Pearce's hayrick to find a place to sleep. That night I had been in trouble with my father and I had told him I would go out. I suddenly thought of a big shed in the yard. When I got inside I found a lot of paper stored in a big heap. I got on top of it and lay down. It was warm and I lighted a cigarette. The lighted match dropped down a parting of the paper to the bottom. It was too narrow for me to get down to put it out and I saw the paper light. It flared up very quickly and to try to put it out, I threw a sack down to try to smother it but it did not do it. I ran from the shed into Cotton Mill-lane the same way as I went in and when I got into the lane, I saw Jim Turvey a lad, I believe he lives in Longmire Road said Pearce's shed is all on fire and there are some cattle inside. I immediately ran along Prospect Road to find a telephone. When half-way along I saw a policeman. I told him of the fire and went back with him to the stile near the allotments in Cotton Mill-lane. I told him there were some cattle in the shed. Later I helped him to get the animals out. I did not tell the policeman that I did it by accident because I was frightened. I did set light to the stack at Kingsbury wilfully but Pearce's fire was an accident.

Evans was judged to be feeble minded under the Mental Deficiencies Act and was committed for twelve months.

Appendix 2
Murder in the Nunnery green space

One of the more exciting stories, gleaned from interviewing Sopwell residents about their early memories, came from Bill Mackenzie. Bill remembers waking up early one December morning in 1948 and looking out of the landing window – he lived in Cottonmill Crescent then – and seeing police vans over at the stables. The stables were where Nunnery Stables is now. Being a young inquisitive lad he went to have a look. He found out that a murder had taken place and that the murdered man's name was Stephen Varley.

The body was found just outside the stables on the allotment side of the fence. Newspaper reports revealed that the body was of fifty-two-year-old Stephen Varley from Watford who worked at de Havilland's in Hatfield as a shop steward. His partly clothed body was found at about 8am on the morning of Sunday 19th December 1948 by Frederick Howe of Bernard Street, one of the allotment holders, who went there to collect some greens for his Sunday lunch.

Stephen Varley, a widower, was described in the *Herts Advertiser* as having been battered about the face and head, apparently on the night before. His body had been carried about a hundred yards along the footpath from the road and dumped by a wicket fence in the shadow of the wall of the ruins. There had been no sign of a struggle. The Chief Constable of Hertfordshire ordered a systematic search to be made of the allotments and of Pearce's dump adjacent to the ruins. Varley's mud-stained shoes were found on an allotment some distance from where his body lay, but the dead man's trousers and jacket could not be found. Four hundred gardeners who had allotments in the area were questioned. Troops searched the golf course. There were several reports from people living in the vicinity of Cottonmill Lane, including one from a youth who said that a group of men had been talking near the river Ver bridge not far from the main entrance gates to the allotments.

Chief Inspector Robert Fabian of Scotland Yard, later of 1950s television fame, was called in to solve the case, as was the eminent forensic pathologist, Dr Keith Simpson. Inspector Bob Fabian of the yard was described as one of Scotland Yard's 'Big Five', the small body of experts who constituted the backbone of the Yard's murder squad.

The police thought a tramp might have picked up Varley's clothes as they were never found. Apparently it was well known that tramps frequented the Nunnery allotments, where they changed into clothes they picked up.

Dr Keith Simpson did the post mortem. He reported that Varley was a heavily built man and physically strong. He had drunk some beer but there was nothing from the examination to show Varley's state of sobriety or otherwise. Injuries were in keeping with Varley having been forced onto his knees or face downwards and having his face, knees and thighs ground in the dirt. The line of his collar band was marked by a deep impression – the result of the collar band being pulled tightly back, causing constriction. On the left side of his neck there were eight fingertip type bruises. It was concluded that death was by constriction. He had also been beaten violently in the face. At the inquest it was revealed that the police interviewed 3,000 people. Amongst those who gave witness statements were Reginald John Smith of 17 Doggetts Way and Arthur James Downey of 1 Cottonmill Close. They both said they had seen him in the company of two men. They had to see his dead body to identify him. Despite every effort to trace the two men who had been drinking with Varley the night before, they were never found and the murder remains unsolved.

Appendix 3
Swimming Baths opening ceremony 1905

The *Herts Advertiser* of 5th August 1905 reported fully on the opening ceremony of the Cottonmill Lane swimming baths which is very important from an historical point of view. The article gives a full picture of the size of the baths and how they were constructed; how the land and funding were obtained and the actual costs; how the water is pumped in and out; the changing facilities; and the important dignitaries present at the ceremony. Interestingly, it also illustrates the urgent need for the swimming baths and for healthy exercise in general 'to counteract the climate of drunkenness and lunacy prevalent at the time'. After the ceremony, a water polo match took place with two local teams.

Baths at last – Leader column

The interesting ceremony in Cotton Mill-Lane on Saturday satisfies, to a large extent, a public grievance of long-standing. For years the need of swimming and other baths has been keenly felt and successive Mayors, stimulated by the earnest appeals of the late Alderman Slade, exercised that influence which they possessed to supply a need which was felt and clamoured for. In this matter, circumstances have dictated the policy. The project is being accomplished step by step, and although the provision made cannot be described as complete, it, at any rate, meets the most pressing need. The absence of swimming accommodation for the youth of the city has been a serious deficiency in our public equipment hitherto. The large bath which has been provided will, we are convinced, be highly appreciated. There is a very satisfactory coincidence in the fact that the son [the Mayor] had been able to achieve the desire of the father [the late Alderman Slade]. The scheme has been judiciously fostered by successive Mayors and the energy and strength of the present Mayor were just what were needed to drive it on to success. One sentence in the graceful little speech of the Mayoress will find response in the heart of every citizen: 'I am sure if one who has passed away [the late Alderman Slade] could be with us it would delight his heart.'

Article

Many sites have, at different times, been before the City Council, but it was finally decided to construct a swimming bath on land belonging to Lord Verulam, situated in Cotton Mill-lane adjacent to the river, and which his lordship agreed to lease to the Corporation for a term of eighty years at a rental of fifteen pounds per annum. In the early spring of this year, the City Surveyor (Mr. Geo. Ford) was instructed to prepare plans for the bath, and on the 10th April a contract was entered into with Mr J. T. Bushell to carry out the work for the sum of £1,275. This sum did not include the engine, pump and means of filling and emptying of the baths. This work has been carried out by the Council's own staff.

The dimensions of the bath are 105 feet by 30 feet at the top water line, at one end and three feet six inches deep at the other. It is constructed of Portland cement concrete walls two feet thick and the bottom one foot thick, the whole being rendered in cement and left with a smooth surface. The footpaths round the bath, which are ten feet wide at the sides and twelve feet at each end, are laid with Imperial stone flags, the whole being surrounded with a brick wall fourteen inches thick and eight feet high, from the path level coped with stone. Twenty-four lock-up dressing boxes, fitted with seats and hat and coat rails are provided. A galvanised iron roof is carried round two sides and one end of the bath, forming a covering for the boxes and shelter for the bathers who do not care to use the boxes. Entrance is effected through a turnstile, and exit is provided by means of another turnstile, also in case of an emergency, by a pair of doors which can only be opened from the inside. The bath is filled from the river, which first flows into a sump through two eight inch iron pipes. It is then pumped by a five inch centrifugal pump to a height of seven feet through a six inch cast iron pipe and delivered into the bath through two openings at the opposite end. Provision is made for emptying by means of a nine inch drain running out of the bottom at the east end of the bath and taken into the river below the bridge. This drain is controlled by a nine inch sluice valve, and there is an overflow box at the surface of the water. The pump is driven by one of Messrs. Crossley's gas engines of five horse power working at 260 revolutions per minute. At this speed it delivers 38,000 gallons of water per hour into the bath and the Surveyor considers that by working the engine one hour each day, sufficient water will be pumped into the bath to entirely change it twice at least each week. The cost of gas for working the engine is estimated at 3 ½d per hour.

The ceremony of publicly opening the baths took place on Saturday, and was one which will leave behind it very pleasant recollections. The day was an ideal one for anything savouring of the aquatic, and there was in consequence a large attendance of members of the Council and their friends, and representative gathering of the general public. Amongst those present were the Mayor and Mayoress (Councillor and Mrs Horace Slade), the Misses Slade, Alderman C. Miskin, Alderman H.P. Smith, Alderman and Mrs Green, Councillor A. Rowden, Councillor and Mrs Ekins, Councillor and the Misses Worssam, Councillor Hodding, Councillor Lee, Councillor Watson, Councillor and Mrs Flint, the Earl of Verulam, Mr H.J. Toulmin, Dr Lipscomb, Mr Thos. Oakley, Mr Henry Watts, Mrs F.R Webster, Mr and Mrs P.C. Blow, Mr J. M. MacLarty, Mr F. Slade, Mr W. Price, Mr W.H. Lavers, Mr C. W. Miskin, Mr A. Miskin, Mr W.G. Marshall, Mr W. Climance, Mr H.Lewis, Mr W. Evans, Mr Carter, Mr J.H. Beatty, Mr G. Ford (City Surveyor), Mr A.E. Slough (Inspector of Weights and Measures) and others.

The Mayor, mounting the diving board at the western end of the baths, was loudly applauded. Addressing himself to the interested gathering he said:

'At last, after many years of anxious inquiry and negotiation, you have tangible proof that the long desired necessity of public baths is an accomplished fact, and I hope that the future of these baths will be as great a success as the making of them has been. I may say that the fact that we are able to have the baths open even this season, comes about through the energy and goodwill of everyone connected with them, and the prompt manner in which they all acted. First of all, the Earl of Verulam, directly the system of pumping the water into the baths was mentioned to him, said: "Take as much land as you require; don't wait for legal formalities, but go on with it at once. I will never put any obstacle in the way of that." (applause) – we never had any opposition in that direction. Then we had a good Town Clerk – (applause) – who hurried on the legal formalities, and meanwhile the City Surveyor got out the plans, so that by the time the lease was signed, all was ready for going on with it; and I think you will agree with me that the builder (Mr J.T. Bushell) has done his work well – (hear, hear). He was right up to time. His time was not up till Thursday, and the baths would have been open then, only other things intervened to prevent it. I think our cordial thanks are due to all those I have named for the hearty way they have entered into it in order to get these baths open this season, although late – (hear, hear). Now for a word as to the future of the baths. Hitherto it has been a reproach that we have not been able to offer any baths in which the people could take recreation or learn swimming. That reproach is certainly now removed, and I hope that all those who come here will use the baths carefully and well and judiciously. There is no doubt whatever that bathing is one of the finest pastimes anyone can indulge in, and I cannot help thinking myself that all outdoor exercise of every description is good, inasmuch as I consider it the greatest antidote possible to drunkenness and lunacy because if the body can be built up and maintained in strength, it is very evident that the brain is kept strengthened also. If that is the case, I am sure we should not have so much drunkenness, neither would our lunatic asylums be so full as they are now if people would devote themselves more largely to these outdoor exercises. I will now ask the Mayoress to declare these baths open for the good and benefit of St Albans (applause).'

The Mayoress, pluckily ascending the steps to the position which his Worship was just about to vacate, was heartily greeted, and with one hand holding the supports of the diving board she said:

'Ladies and Gentlemen, I have very great pleasure in declaring these baths open for the use of the public, and I hope we may soon see many of the young people indulging in swimming and giving us a sight of their prowess in that subject (applause). I am sure if one who has passed away could be with us it would delight his heart.'

Appendix 4
Sopwell Mill fire 1883

This is the article in the *Herts Advertiser* of 27th October 1883 which reported the fire at Sopwell Mill. The description of the extent of the fire is extremely detailed so we can imagine what the mill and the adjoining house were like at the time. The Fire Brigade going to the wrong location and the theft of the fowls is quite amusing.

Destructive fire at St Albans: a mill destroyed

A fire which was the cause of a considerable amount of damage occurred in the neighbourhood of St Albans on Monday night. The scene of the outbreak was Sopwell Mill in the occupation of Mr Edmund Hinton. The property which belongs to the Earl of Verulam is situate near the Sopwell Nunnery, and lies just outside the city boundary, the lines of the London and North Western and Great Northern Railway Companies bordering it on either side. The mill was only three years since thoroughly renovated and new machinery was put in, so that its destruction at this period is particularly unfortunate. Mr Hinton has been tenant of the property for some 15 or 16 years. The dwelling house, in which he and Mrs Hinton resided, immediately adjoins the mill, and there was a passage way from which direct access could be obtained from the one to the other. The mill is supplied with two pairs of stones. On Monday not a great amount of work was done during the day, the water being rather slack, but towards evening the speed was increased. Work was continued until nine o'clock, at which time Mr Hinton locked up the mill, leaving everything in an apparently safe condition. The only light which had been used there was a small paraffin lamp, which Mr Hinton brought with him from the mill, and which appears to have burnt so low that it was blown out by the wind as he was bringing it into the house. Nobody had been smoking on the premises, and the absence of this and other ordinary grounds of explanation leaves the origin of the conflagration something of a mystery. It was about ten o'clock that the flames were discovered. Mr and Mrs Hinton had retired to rest for the night when they were awakened by hearing a crackling noise. On coming down the mill was discovered to be in a perfect blaze, and the fire was rapidly making its way to the house. Considering its quick progress it was very fortunate that Mr and Mrs Hinton were awoke so early. As it was there was barely time for them to escape in safety. The room in which they slept was in immediate proximity to the mill, and so rapid was the spread of the fire that by the time they got out the roof covering the room was in flames, and the lower part of the premises threatened to be speedily consumed. Mrs Hinton had to leave the house with little or no clothes. The engine driver and guard of a goods train, which was proceeding on the Great Northern Railway towards Hatfield , observed the conflagration and gave an alarm, they, next to Mr Hinton himself, being almost the earliest to notice the outbreak. Very opportunely also Mr F. Silvester, of Hedges Farm, was at the time driving along the lane towards home, and he kindly conveyed Mrs Hinton to his farm, where she, together with her husband, by whom she was afterwards joined, found a hospitable shelter. Meanwhile a messenger was sent off for the Fire Brigade. The men of the county force, under the direction of Capt. Seymour, were the first on the spot, having reached thither and got to work a considerable time before the city men put in an appearance. The reason of the apparent tardiness of the latter was accounted for by a most awkward piece of bungling on the part of those by whom the call was made. Only two or three of the city men seem to have been apprised at all. The captain (Mr Thorpe) was not called, and in some other instances the men had no notification of the event. Those who did hear anything about it were erroneously informed that the fire was at Mr Pinnock's sheds, and acting on this information they, with promptitude, ran down with the hose-reel only to find that it was so much labour lost, and that the conflagration was at another place. They returned with the reel, and subsequently took down the engine, running it there by hand. When eventually they got to work their efforts backing up those of the County men soon had a material effect on staying the progress of the flames. Sergt. Smith arrived at 11.30 and took over the command of the City men. Water was obtained from the adjacent river and was poured on the fire in copious quantities. The mill was completely destroyed and now with its damaged machinery, broken girders and twisted bars, presents the appearance of a perfect wreck, the only thing remaining intact in its original position being the large driving-wheel which, being outside was fortunately saved from destruction by an intervening wall. The bedroom in which Mr Hinton was sleeping was, together with the room beneath, burnt out. The books, which kept in a small office leading out from the kitchen, were fortunately secured in time. The furniture in the other parts of the house was likewise rescued, but the contents of the bedroom were completely destroyed, including a considerable quantity of clothes which were in the cupboard. The roof at the end nearest the mill has fallen in, but the progress of the flames at the back of the house and towards the part nearest the stable was prevented. The contents of the back kitchen remain intact, even to a copy of the *Herts Advertiser* Almanack hanging from the wall, but the from apartment presents a sorry plight. Fearing the spread of the flames in the direction of the stable, Mr Hinton caused his two horses to be removed. The stable, however, was in no way attacked, being used afterwards as a storing place for the furniture. Willing hands were found to assist in the work of the removal. Some, however, there were who carried their activity a trifle too far, and did not stop even at felony. There were about 60 fowls in a small house adjoining the mill, and, acting in a most impudent way, some dishonest persons present went in and helped themselves. So extensive was the peculation that out of the 60 fowls, there were after the fire there only about a dozen-and-half, dead and alive, remaining. There were also 16 or 17 ducks, and of these several are missing. Some County policemen were on the spot during the night, but do not seem to have captured any of the thieves. The City engine remained until about half-past one. All danger was past by midnight, but it was of course necessary to continue playing on the smouldering materials, for some considerable time longer, and the County engine remained for that purpose until eight o'clock on Tuesday morning, playing at intervals where necessary.. The reflection of the fire could be seen for a considerable distance, and the crackling of the timber was also heard a long way off, the woodwork being very dry and burning with great rapidity. Mr J. Purrott, agent for the Earl of Verulam, visited the scene on Tuesday morning and made an inspection, as did also the representatives of the insurance offices concerned. In the evening, the County brigade were called to the scene to extinguish another small outbreak. The buildings, machinery etc., belonging to the landlord are fully insured in the Phoenix Office, the local agent for which is Mr J. Robertson. It is estimated that the damage to the buildings, etc., amounts to about £800. Mr Hinton is insured in the County Office (agent, Mr Charles Harris) for £800, of which £200 was for goods in trusts for customers and on commission. Within the latter category will come 40 quarters of barley which was destroyed in the mill, this belonging to Mr Cole, of Hemel Hempstead. There was also a considerable quantity of flour in the mill, which together with the other contents was burned. Altogether the damage is very considerable and much sympathy is expressed for Mr and Mrs Hinton, who are people well advanced in years. The earl of Verulam, Viscount Grimston and Lady Harriot Grimston called on Mr Hinton on Wednesday and gave expression to the sympathy which they felt for them.

Author's endnote and acknowledgements

This may be the end of the book but really it is just the beginning. There are, of course, many more stories to be told and memories to be collected. The Sopwell Project will continue and anyone else wishing to tell their story may contact the Sopwell Residents Association. It has to be borne in mind that the memories collected from residents are personal. Others may have a different memory of similar events.

There are many people to acknowledge. First of all, I must thank those who believed in us and gave contributions to get this work in print: Martin Frearson our county councillor for the Herts County Council Locality grant; the Ver Valley Society, Verulam Golf Club, Pearce Recycling, Edgar Pearce and Blacks of Sopwell for their generous contributions; and Kate Bretherton for agreeing to be our publisher.

Grateful thanks must go to my colleagues on the SRA committee, especially Chris Pudsey for her environmental and copy-editing expertise, and Rob Sharman for working out all the 'hard sums'. I must thank Anne Wares for all her research on the history of Priory Park and New Barnes; Eileen Harris for all her help and research in starting me off on this journey; Steve Peters for his research and photographs; and to all those residents who came forward to contribute their memories: Nancy Broadbent, Margaret Brown, Dorothea Bristow, John Buckingham, Winnie Day, Lil Day, Gerald Dunham, Pauline Crosier, Betty Cutler, Tom Edgar, Irene Ewer, Vic and Vera Foster, Alfie Francis, Joan Forder, Bobby Jones, Pamela Marshall, Bill Mackenzie, Kathy Sinfield, Betty Terry and Margaret Wickens. Thanks must also go to Andy Webb of the Ver Valley Society, Mark and Rebecca Boxer, Graham Elliott, Fred Edwards, Barbara Thomason, the library at the St Albans and Hertfordshire Architectural and Archaeological Society (SAHAAS or the 'Arc and Arc'), Elanor Cowland and the St Albans Museum service, St Adrian's school, Mandeville School and Verulam Golf Club.

I must also thank all those who provided me with images to use in this book especially, those obtained from the St Albans Museum collection. It was difficult deciding what to leave out. Especially relevant were the prints by J.H. Buckingham who painted many beautiful watercolours from the Sopwell area. He must have loved Sopwell as much as we do.

Sandy Norman

Memory contributors

In order to put the memories of living in Sopwell in a timeframe, here are brief biographies of those residents who have kindly contributed their memories.

- Nancy Broadbent was born in St Albans in 1949 and moved with her family to Creighton Avenue in 1952.
- Margaret Brown, born 1923, has lived on the Mentmore estate since she was eleven.
- John Buckingham was born in 1943 and has lived in Sopwell all his life, as did his father.
- Betty Cutler was born in 1923 in St Albans. In 1930, aged seven, she and her family moved to Cottonmill.
- Lil Day and her husband moved into their new council house in Priory Walk after the war. Her daughter Pauline Crosier was born in 1947.
- Winnie Day, born 1925, lived on the Watford Road until she moved to Sopwell in 1950.

- Gerald Dunham was born in St Albans in 1934. He moved into Longmire Road in the 1960s.
- Tom Edgar's in-laws, the Millmans, lived in Tavistock Avenue from 1937 until the 1980s.
- Joan Forder went to school with Kathy Sinfield and lived in Sopwell until she was 17.
- Vic Foster was born in 1941 and moved to Cottonmill in 1947. His wife Vera, born 1942, lived in Cottonmill from 1949 to 53.
- Alfie Francis was born 1932 in London. His family moved to a new house in Gorham Drive after the war.
- Bobby Jones, born in 1943, moved into a new house in Pemberton Close with her parents in 1950 and has remained in Sopwell ever since.
- Bill Mackenzie was born in 1939. His family moved to Cottonmill in 1942.
- Pamela Marshall was born in 1943. Her family moved to their new council house in Berners Drive in 1948 when she was five.
- Kathy Sinfield was born in 1929. Her family moved into Doggetts Way when she was about four years old.
- Betty Terry 1919–2011. Her family moved to Sopwell Gate Lodge, Cottonmill Lane in 1929. In 1933–34, her family moved to Vesta Avenue where she lived until the war. Betty unfortunately passed away before this book was published.
- Margaret Wickens was born in Old London Road in 1933 and moved to Ramsbury Road during the war.

About the author

Sandy Norman has lived in Tavistock Avenue since 1971. She is a Chartered Librarian and a Fellow and Honorary Fellow of the Chartered Institute of Library and Information Professionals (CILIP). She has been actively involved in the Sopwell Residents Association since its inception in 2003.

Selective bibliography

Andrews, J. & Wren, M., *A plan of the town of St Albans in Hartfordshire*, London, A. Dury, 1766.

Andrews, P.G., *A brief chronicle of the first Twenty-five years of the Abbeyfield St Albans Society*, 1985.

Ashdown, Charles H. & Kitton, Frederick, *St Albans: Historical and Picturesque*, Elliot Stock, London, 1893.

Catt, John, *Hertfordshire Geology and Landscape*, Hertfordshire Natural History Society, 2010, 978-0-9521685-9-1.

Cussons, John, A Professional Hertfordshire Tramp <u>in</u> *Hertfordshire Record Publications, Vol. 3*, 1987.

Dunn, George & Dunn, Carrie, *From the Valleys to Verulamium*, The History Press, 2011, 9 780752 465081.

Fookes, Michael, *Made in St Albans*, Michael Fookes, 1987, 0 9528861 0 3.

Freeman, Mark, *St Albans: a history*, Carnegie Publishing, 2008, 978-1-85836-139-9.

Fry, Peter, *Verulam Golf Club 1905–2005*, 2006.

Gibbs, A.E., *Historical records of St Albans*, 1888.

Gibbs, A.E., *The corporation records of St Albans, 1890.*

Green, John Richard, *A short history of the English People* (Peasants Revolt Pt V – available online).

Haynes, Tony 1986,
  <u>In</u> http://people.bath.ac.uk/liskmj/living-spring/sourcearchive/fs6/fs6th1.htm

Herts Advertiser

Hertfordshire houses: a selective inventory, Royal Commission on the historic monuments of England, 1993, 1873592108.

History of the County of Hertford, Vol. 2, *British History Online,* 1908, http://www.british-history.ac.uk/report.aspx?compid=43303#n81.

Hospitals: St Julian by St Albans, *A History of the County of Hertford: Volume 4* (1971), pp. 464–467.

Kelly's directories.

Lansberry, H.C.F., St Albans Canal <u>in</u> *Herts Past and Present,* 1968.

Lewis, Samuel, *Topographical Dictionary of England,* 1842.

Marshall, Pamela, *The Taylor Family of Cottonmill 1948–1965*, Unpublished.

Mercer, Tony, *Mercer Chronometers: History, Maintenance and Repair,* Mayfield Books, 2003.

Moody, Brian, *SAHAAS Newsletter* No. 168, May 2008.

Niblett, Rosalind & Thompson, Isobel, *Alban's buried towns*, Oxbow books, 2005, 1-84217-149-6.

Roach, Anne & Wheeler, Matthew, *St Albans: the home front,* St Albans Museums, 1995.

Roberts, Eileen, *St Albans Borough Boundary*, 1980.

Taylor, Roger D. & Anderson, Brian, *The Hatfield and St Albans Branch of the Great Northern Railway*, Oakwood Press, 1988, 0 85361 373 7.

Saturday afternoon rambles for pedestrians no. 5 St Albans to Harpenden, The *Daily News*, Saturday 7th July 1900, p.6.

St Albans District Council draft Conservation and Character statement Area 20, September 2010.

St Albans Review.

Ver Valley Society letters 1987 (available in St Albans library).

Wares, Anne, *A history of Priory Park*, 2004.

Williams, *St Albans,* 1820.

References

1. It is likely Sopwell Mill is New Barnes Mill and Stankfield is Sopwell Mill!
2. History of the County of Hertford, Vol 2, *British History Online* 1908 http://www.british-history.ac.uk/report.aspx?compid=43303#n81
3. Gibbs, A.E., *Historical records of St Albans*, 1888
4. *ibid.*
5. Hospitals: St Julian by St Albans In *A History of the County of Hertford: Volume 4* (1971)
6. Gibbs *op. cit.*
7. *Dictionary of National Biography*
8. Gibbs *op. cit.*
9. Gibbs *op. cit.*
10. Niblett, Rosalind, and Thompson, Isobel. *Alban's Buried Towns*
11. Ashdown, Charles, *St Albans Historical and Picturesque*
12. Wares, Anne, *A history of Priory Park*, 2004
13. http://www.salbani.co.uk/Med%20Web/churches.htm
14. Ashdown *op. cit.*
15. Simon West
16. History of the County of Hertford *op. cit.*
17. Ashdown *op. cit.*
18. *St Albans and West Herts News*, January 1890
19. Interview with Steve Peters from an article in the *Herts Advertiser* in 1929
20. Ashdown *op. cit.*
21. Roberts, Eileen, *Saint Alban's Borough Boundary*, 1980
22. Williams, *St Albans,* 1820
23. Niblett and Thompson *op. cit.*
24. Ashdown *op. cit.*
25. Haynes, Tony 1986, In http://people.bath.ac.uk/liskmj/living-spring/sourcearchive/fs6/fs6th1.htm
26. *ibid.*
27. *ibid.*
28. *Review,* 14th June 1984
29. *Review,* 4th October 1984
30. Niblett and Thompson o*p. cit.*
31. Ashdown *op. cit.*
32. St Stephen's Church pamphlet, The story of the Dunkeld lectern
33. Most of this chapter was researched and written by Anne Wares
34. *Hertfordshire houses: a selective inventory*
35. *ibid.*
36. *ibid.*
37. Andrews, P.G., *The Abbeyfield St Albans Society*
38. Roft, Derek. The house in the middle of the road. www.hertsmemories.org.uk
39. Ver Valley Society
40. Green, John Richard, *A short history of the English people*
41. Cussons, John, *A professional Hertfordshire tramp*
42. Lewis, Samuel, *Topographical Dictionary of England, 1842*
43. Cussons *op. cit.*
44. *Universal Directory of British Trade and Commerce, Vol. 5*
45. Pigot's Directories
46. F.A.J. Harding, The church in the cotton mill In *Hertfordshire Countryside,* Autumn 1951
47. Cussons *op. cit.*
48. Gibbs, A.E., *Corporation records of St Albans.* 1890
49. Ashdown, Charles and Kitton, Frederick, *St Albans Historical and Picturesque*
50. Green, Judy, *Little Ver Book,* Ver Valley Society, 1992
51. Henry Norris miller, Sopwell Mill registered will 13AR66. HALS
52. Deeds (XIII/49) HALS
53. This was later known as the Wendover Arm, part of the Grand Union Canal
54. Fookes, Michael, *Made in St Albans*
55. www.independent.co.uk
56. Fookes *op. cit.*

[57] Reference to the Plan of a proposed Navigable Cut from the Town of Watford in the County of Hertford to the town of St Albans in the same County, QS Highway Diversions 495c. Held in HALS. Information also found in the tithe maps.

[58] Little Sopwell Farm – plan, report, correspondence D/EV/E82 in HALS

[59] St Albans St Michaels Manorial Field Book D/EV/M39 1766-7 in HALS

[60] Hedges and Sopwell Farms – lease for 21 years D/EV/E80 in HALS

[61] Joanne Pearce correspondence 2010

[62] http://www.salbani.co.uk/Med%20Web/outside_the_town.htm

[63] Lansberry, H.C.F., St Albans Canal In *Herts Past and Present,* 1968

[64] *ibid.*

[65] *ibid.*

[66] Catt, John, *Hertfordshire Geology and Landscape*

[67] *ibid.*

[68] Gibbs, A.E., *The corporation records of St Albans, 1890*

[69] Taylor, Roger D. and Anderson, Brian, *The Hatfield and St Albans Branch of the Great Northern Railway*

[70] *ibid.*

[71] Fookes *op. cit.*

[72] Fookes *op. cit.*

[73] Fookes *op. cit.*

[74] Fookes *op. cit.*

[75] Kathy Sinfield interview 10th November 2010

[76] *Herts Advertiser* 27th July 1951

[77] Mercer, Tony, *Mercer chronometers: history, maintenance and repair*

[78] Fookes *op. cit.*

[79] Mercer *op. cit.*

[80] Freeman, Mark, *St Albans: a history*

[81] Cussons, John, *A professional Hertfordshire tramp*

[82] *Daily News* Tues 25th May 1886

[83] Joanne Pearce correspondence 2010

[84] St Albans Museum oral history collection interview with Alfred Bacon

[85] Fookes *op. cit.*

[86] Fookes *op. cit.*

[87] Moody, Brian, *SAHAAS Newsletter* No. 168, May 2008

[88] *Herts Advertiser,* 31st January 1986

[89] St Albans District Council draft Conservation and Character statement Area 10, September 2010

[90] Ashdown *op. cit.*

[91] Gardiner, Jean, A most moving road, *Herts Advertiser* 8th November 1984

[92] Kelly's Directory of St Albans 1938–9

[93] Wares *op. cit.*

[94] Papers held at Hertfordshire Libraries and Archives: D/EV/E94

[95] *ibid.* D/EV/E101

[96] St Albans District Council draft Conservation and Character statement Area 20, September 2010

[97] *ibid.*

[98] *ibid.*

[99] *ibid.*

[100] Wares, Anne gives a fuller history of Priory Park in her booklet: *A history of Priory Park*

[101] Wares *op. cit.*

[102] *ibid.*

[103] *ibid.*

[104] *ibid.*

[105] http://www.stalbansband.co.uk/band-history/26-memories-from-george-wright.html

[106] Saturday afternoon rambles for pedestrians, no. 5 St Albans to Harpenden, *The Daily News* July 1900

[107] County Chronicle, 15th September 1818, p.3

[108] Kelly's Directories 1924–32

[109] Kelly's Directory 1906

[110] *Herts Advertiser,* April 1932

[111] Andrews P.G., *A brief chronicle of the first Twenty-five years of the Abbeyfield St Albans Society,* 1985

[112] Wares *op. cit.*

[113] Roach Anne and Wheeler Matthew, *St Albans: the home front,* St Albans Museums, 1995

[114] *Herts Advertiser,* 27th August 1948

[115] *Herts Advertiser,* 28th October 1948

[116] Dunn, George and Dunn, Carrie, *From the Valleys to Verulamium*
[117] *Herts Advertiser,* 23rd November 1951
[118] *Herts Advertiser,* 8th October 1948
[119] St Peter's School website http://www.stpeters.herts.sch.uk/our_school/history.html
[120] *ibid.*
[121] *ibid.*
[122] St Albans Almanac 1882
[123] *Herts Advertiser,* 7th September 1951
[124] http://www.parishonline.co.uk/church/content/pages/about-us.php
[125] *Herts Advertiser,* 1st February 1952
[126] *Herts Advertiser* 30th May 1952
[127] Philip Norcross, Secretary Christadelphian Church, Abbots Avenue
[128] http://www.saint-barts.info/SbStoryChurch.html
[129] *ibid.*
[130] Fry Peter, *Verulam Golf Club 1905–2005.*
[131] Verulam Golf Club Centenary brochure, 2005.
[132] Letter to Ver Valley Society 1987, from Mr Golding
[133] *Herts Advertiser,* 1883
[134] *St Albans and W. Herts News,* August 1890
[135] Letter from Tadpole *Herts Advertiser,* 10th July 1932
[136] Ver Valley Society review of 1977
[137] Letter to Ver Valley Society, 21st February 1987, from Miss Blowers
[138] *Herts Advertiser,* 29th February 1980
[139] Letter to Ver Valley Society, 1987, from William Goodman
[140] *St Albans and West Herts News,* January 1891
[141] Golding *op. cit.*
[142] Golding *op. cit.*
[143] Golding *op. cit.*
[144] Letter to Ver Valley Society, 1987, from Mrs Murray
[145] *ibid.*
[146] www.verulam-angling.co.uk
[147] Jennifer Taylor
[148] *Review,* 6th May 1976
[149] Dunn and Dunn o*p.cit.*
[150] *Review,* 17th April 1975
[151] *Herts Advertiser,* 5th May 1989 p.3
[152] Anne Wares interview with Gerry Dunham, February 2002

Index